Love

& Its Meaning in the World

Love

& Its Meaning in the World

Selected Lectures and Writings

RUDOLF STEINER

Anthroposophic Press

Published by Anthroposophic Press
3390 Route 9, Hudson, NY 12534

Library of Congress Cataloging-in-Publication Data

Steiner, Rudolf, 1861–1925.
[Selections. English. 1998]
Love & its meaning in the world : selected lectures and writings / Rudolf Steiner.
p. cm.
Includes bibliographical references
Contents: The division of the sexes -- Lucifer and Christ -- The mission of reverence -- Love, the mission of the earth I -- Love, the mission of the earth II -- Love, the mission of the earth III -- The Buddha's teaching of compassion and love -- Faith, hope, love I -- Faith, hope, love II -- Love and its meaning in the world.
ISBN 0-88010-441-4
1. Love--Religious aspects. 2. Anthroposophy. I. Title.
BP596.L67S74213 1998
299'.935--dc21 98-30549
CIP

10 9 8 7 6 5 4 3 2 1

Printed in the United States of America.

Sources

The following have been newly translated or thoroughly revised and edited by the publisher: "The Mystery of Love" from *Christianity as Mystical Fact*, trans., Andrew Welburn (*Das Christentum als mystische Tatsache und die Mysterien des Altertums*, Rudolf Steiner Verlag, Dornach, Switzerland, GA 8); "The Division into Sexes" from *Cosmic Memory*, trans., Karl E. Zimmer (*Aus der Akasha-Chronik*, GA 11); "Lucifer, the Bearer of Light" and "The Children of Lucifer" from *The Christian Mystery*, trans., James Hindes (*Das christliche Mysterium*, GA 97); "The Mission of Reverence" from *Metamorphoses of the Soul*, vol. 1, trans., C. Davy & C. von Arnim (*Metamorphosen des Seelenlebens: Pfade der Seelenerlebnisse*, GA 58); "Love: the Mission of the Earth I" from *The Gospel of St. John*, trans., Maud B. Monges (*Das Johannes-Evangelium*, GA 103); "Love: the Mission of the Earth II" from *Universe, Earth and Man* (*Welt, Erde und Mensch*, GA 105); "Love: the Mission of the Earth III" from *Earthly and Cosmic Man* (*Der irdische und der kosmische Mensch*, GA 133); "The Buddha's Teaching of Compassion and Love" from *The Gospel of St. Luke*, trans., D.S. Osmond (*Das Lukas-Evangelium*, GA 114); "Faith, Love, Hope" I & II from *Faith, Love, Hope* (*Das esoterische Christentum und die geistige Führung der Menschheit*, GA 130); "Freedom and Love," extract of a lecture from *The Apocalypse of St. John* (*Die Apokalypse des Johannes*, GA 104) "Love and Its Meaning in the World," trans., D.S. Osmond. & E.F. & S. Derry (*Erfahrungen des Übersinnlichen: Die Wege der Seele zu Christus*, GA 143); Epilogue: "I-Feeling, the Human Soul's Capacity to Love, and Their Relationship to the Elementary World" and other extracts from *The Threshold of the Spiritual World* (*Ein Weg zur Selbsterkenntnis des Menschen*, GA 16); three prayers for the dead, trans., C. Bamford from *Unsere Toten*, (GA 261); verse on p. 8, "für Johanna Mücke" trans., C. Bamford from *Wahrspruchworte* (GA 40).

Contents

In the heart—
a human organ
of all organs
containing matter
more spiritual
than any other.

In the heart—
matter revealing
spirit more
than any other.

In the heart—
the Sun
in the human universe.

In the heart—
we are
closest
to the deepest
source of our being.

Rudolf Steiner

Introduction

> For human beings, love is the most important fruit of experience in the sense world. Once we really understand the nature of love, or compassion, we will find that love is the way spirit expresses its truth in the world of the senses....
>
> We may even say that, in love, the spiritual world awakens in the physical. The more truly a soul inhabits the spiritual worlds, the more it experiences lovelessness and lack of compassion as a denial of spirit itself.
>
> —Rudolf Steiner, Aphorism 9
> *The Threshold of the Spiritual World*

ALTHOUGH Rudolf Steiner does not often speak or write of love explicitly, love is the very heart and ground of all his teaching, the foundation of all he did, and all he hoped that we would do.

Love of humanity (the living and the so-called dead), the Earth, the cosmos, and the Divine motivated all that he accomplished, his enormous life work. In the final chapter of his basic work on inner development, *How To Know Higher Worlds*, he speaks of meeting with the Greater Guardian of the Threshold after one has achieved liberation from the world of the senses and the ability to work freely in the world of the supersensible.

> Now that you are free, [the Guardian says] you can help free all your fellow beings in the sense world. Up to now you have striven as an individual. Now you must join yourself to the whole, so that you may bring with you into the supersensible realm not only yourself but also all else that exists in the sensible world. (p. 203)

Steiner comments:

> Should we therefore decide to meet the demands of this higher being of light, we will be able to contribute to the liberating of the human race. We will then offer up our gifts and talents on the sacrificial altar of humanity. (p. 204)

Anthroposophy, the science of the spirit Rudolf Steiner inaugurated, is the living testament of this primacy of love, and rests upon it.

Steiner teaches that, without love, nothing is possible; but that, with love, we can do everything. Love is always love of the not-yet. To love is to create; it is to enter selflessly into the current of time that flows toward us from the future.

Love, in fact, is the mission of the Earth. It is the task of human beings to transubstantiate its wisdom, the very substance of the Earth, into love. For this reason, the Buddha taught compassion. For this reason, Christ through His death and resurrection entered the Earth as love made flesh to become the Spirit of the Earth and the guardian of humanity—to the end of time. Through our wonder, love, and conscience, we build up His body.

Reality, true knowledge of reality, is impossible without love. Only through love can we truly know as we are known, can we encounter the world and its beings in a living way. Without love, knowledge becomes manipulation, domination, control; the world becomes a space of dead things. But, when we know through love, we enter into a pattern of dynamic, potentially redemptive relations and the world becomes a *living* world of beings working for the good.

But it is not only our cognitive relations that rest on love—although, of course, cognition is cardinal in all our thinking, feeling, and willing. Love also makes healthy social and political relations possible. Steiner's "threefold social order," for instance, clearly depends upon love. In his call for a new form of society, Steiner called upon human beings to exercise mutual freedom in the spiritual sphere, equality in the rights sphere, and brotherhood/sisterhood in the economic sphere. But these ideals of freedom, equality, and brotherhood/sisterhood are unrealizable without love—understood here as the overcoming of egotism, as the ability to die to self and live for, and in, the other. Waldorf education, too, depends upon the teachers' ability to love their students: without that love, education is impossible. Whenever he went to visit the first Waldorf school, Rudolf Steiner would always ask the children, "Do you *love* your teachers?" The teachers, he didn't have to ask: he assumed they did. Indeed, Steiner assumed this primacy of love in everything he did and asked others to do.Without the fundamental, ontological, and epistemological commitment to the embodied practice of love, nothing is possible: no agriculture, no medicine, no arts, no sciences, no society, no community, no true human beings.

Why, then, did Rudolf Steiner not talk and write more about love?

First, perhaps, because he took the primacy of love for granted and knew that it was implicit in everything he said and did—in his whole worldview of cosmic and human evolution. And second, perhaps, just because he knew that love is so fundamental, so basic, so nearly identical with the transcendental nature of humanity and the Earth itself, he felt that it could not be addressed directly but only implied, stammered toward, and alluded to. Third, a moment's reflection reveals that nothing is less understood or more misunderstood than love; and that it is both something that everyone feels he or she is an expert in and something that is bound up with conflicting and unconscious wishes and desires at all levels. Therefore, to speak of it directly in any other setting than the most intimate is to run the risk of serious miscommunication and worse. For this reason, again, the indirect approach would seem the most appropriate.

This said, we have gathered together in this volume a number of Steiner's most explicit statements on love and its meaning.

The reader will find here intimations of the meaning of love from the most varied points of view.

Christopher Bamford

PROLOGUE

The Mystery of Love

from *Christianity as Mystical Fact*

PLATO'S "dialogue on love," the *Symposium*, describes an "initiation." In this initiation, love appears as the herald of wisdom. If wisdom, the eternal Word or *Logos*, is the Son of the eternal world creator, then love has a motherly relationship with this Logos.

Before a bright spark of the light of wisdom can flash forth in the human soul, there must exist a darker longing, a tug toward the divine. We must be drawn unconsciously toward what later, raised into consciousness, will constitute our highest joy. What appears in Heraclitus as the "daemon," the higher self, is thus united with the idea of love.[1]

---

1. "...The spirit works in human beings. But it works in them in a special way—out of the temporal. It is our special characteristic as human beings that something in time works like something eternal, that, in time, it leads and enables like something eternal. This characteristic makes us at once like gods and like worms. We are placed midway between god and animal. But this leading and enabling power in us we may call our *daimon*. The *daimon* is what in us strives to go beyond us. As Heraclitus strikingly puts it, "A person's *daimon* is his or her destiny." (*Daimon* is here used in the Greek sense. In the modern sense we would say "spirit.")" From *Christianity as Mystical Fact*, chapter 2.

In the *Symposium*, people of the most varied kinds, with very different opinions on life, speak of love: the ordinary person, the politician, the scientist, the comic poet Aristophanes, and the serious poet Agathon. Each has a view of love appropriate to their life experience. The ways they express themselves reveal the developmental stage of their *daemon* or eternal self.

One being is drawn to another through love. The manifold variety and multiplicity of things, into which divine unity is diffused, strives toward oneness and harmony through love. Love, therefore, has a divine quality, and each person can understand it only to the degree that he or she participates in this divine quality.

After these speakers, who represent various stages of maturity, have declared their views on love, Socrates takes up the discussion. He considers love as a cognitive being, a thinker. For Socrates, love is no god—love is what *leads* human beings to God. *Eros,* love, is not a god for him. God is perfect, and therefore has beauty and goodness. Eros is only the longing for beauty and goodness. Eros therefore *stands between* human beings and God. Love is a *daemon,* a mediator between the earthly and the heavenly.

It is important that, when he speaks of love, Socrates does not claim to give his *own* thoughts. In this regard, Socrates says he will tell only what a woman has given him as a *revelation.* Thus Socrates has come to an idea of love's nature through the art of prophecy. Diotima, the priestess, woke up what, as the daemonic force within him, would lead Socrates to the Divine. She "initiated" him.

This feature of the *Symposium* speaks volumes. We must ask, Who is this "wise woman" who awakens the daemon in Socrates? We should not think this is mere poetic machinery. No actual, physical wise woman could have awakened the daemon in Socrates' soul if the force for such awakening were not within the soul itself. We must therefore seek this "wise woman" in the soul of Socrates himself. But there must be a reason why what brings the daemon to existence in Socrates' soul appears as an outwardly real being. This force cannot work in the same way as the forces we can observe in the soul that belong to it and feel at home there. We see that it is the force of the soul before it has received wisdom, which Socrates represents as the "wise woman." It is the *maternal* principle that gives birth to the Son of God, Wisdom, the Logos.

The unconscious active force of the soul is presented as a feminine element that allows the Divine to enter consciousness. The soul, still without wisdom, is the mother of what leads to the Divine. This leads us to an important idea of mysticism. The soul is recognized as the mother of the Divine. With the inevitability of a natural force, it *unconsciously* leads human beings toward the Divine....

The world of the gods is born in the soul. We look upon what we ourselves create in the form of images as our gods.[2] But we must advance to another idea. The divine power within us, which is active before we create the images of the gods, must also be transformed into a divine image. Thus, behind the Divine, appears the mother of the Divine. She is none other than the original power of the human soul. Beside the gods, we place the goddesses.

Consider the myth of Dionysos, the son of Zeus and Semele, a mortal mother. Semele is struck by lightning. Zeus tears the premature infant, Dionysos, from his mother's womb, and hides him in his own thigh until he is mature. Hera, the mother

2. See *Christianity as Mystical Fact,* pp. 17–21.

of the gods, stirs up the Titans against Dionysos. They dismember the boy. But Pallas Athene saves his still-beating heart and brings it to Zeus. He begets his son a second time. This myth gives us an exact description of a process that occurs in the depths of the human soul.

Like the Egyptian priest who instructed Solon about the nature of a myth, one could say: When you tell us that Dionysos, the son of a god and a mortal mother, is dismembered and then born again, it may sound like a fable; but its truth expresses the birth of the Divine and its destiny in the human soul. The Divine unites with the temporal, earthly human soul. As soon as the divine element Dionysos is revived, the soul experiences a tremendous longing for its true spiritual form. The consciousness appears again in the image of a female divinity, Hera, and becomes jealous of that birth from a superior consciousness. It stirs the lower human nature—the Titans.

The child of god, still immature, is dismembered. It is present in humanity as a dismembered materialistic and intellectual science. But if enough higher wisdom (Zeus) is active in human beings, it cherishes and cares for the immature child, which is then born again as the second son of god (Dionysos). Thus, out of science—out of the dismembered divine force in humanity—is born the harmonizing wisdom, which is the Logos, the son of God and a mortal mother, the transitory human soul striving unconsciously toward the Divine.

We are far from the spiritual reality in all this if we recognize in it only psychological processes—and merely pictures of such processes, at that. In this spiritual reality, the soul does not merely experience something within itself; rather, it is completely disconnected from itself and participates in a cosmic process that in fact happens outside itself and not within it.

1.
The Division into Sexes

from *Cosmic Memory*

THE human male and female forms developed over the course of time from a more ancient, basic form, in which human beings were neither one nor the other, but both at once. In order to understand these enormously distant periods of the past, we must free ourselves completely of what we see around us.

We will look back into a time that existed somewhat before the middle of the epoch we have termed the *Lemurian*. The human body then still consisted of soft and pliable materials. The other forms of Earth also were still soft and pliable. In contrast to its later more hardened condition, Earth still flowed and was fluid. As the human soul was at that time becoming embodied in matter, it was able to adapt matter to itself much more than it could later on. The soul assumes a male or a female body, since one or the other is forced on it through the development of outer, physical nature. When the material substances had not yet become rigid, the soul could force them to obey its own laws, and it made the body as an impression of its own nature.

As matter became more dense, however, the soul had to submit to the laws impressed on matter by natural, earthly processes. As long as the soul could still control matter, it formed its body as neither male nor female, instead giving it qualities that embraced both at the same time. For the soul is simultaneously both male and female; it carries these two natures in itself. The male element is related to what we call *will,* the female element to *imagination.*

The outer formation of the Earth caused the body to assume a one-sided form. The male body took a form conditioned by the element of will; the female body, on the other hand, bears the stamp of imagination. Thus it came about that the double-sexed (both male and female) soul inhabits a single-sexed (male *or* female) body. As the body developed, it assumed a form determined by outer, earthly forces; thus, the soul was no longer able to pour its whole energy into the body. The soul had to retain some of its energy within itself, allowing only part of it to flow into the body.

Continuing with the Akashic Chronicle, something else becomes apparent. During an ancient period, the human forms appearing to us are soft and pliable—very different from those that appear later. They still carry the nature of both man and woman equally within themselves. But with time, the material substances become denser, and the human body appears in two forms: one begins to resemble the subsequent shape of a man, the other that of a woman. Before this difference appeared, any human being could reproduce out of itself. Impregnation did not occur externally, but was initiated with the human body. By becoming male *or* female, the body lost the ability to self-impregnate and had to act together with another body to produce a new human being.

The division into sexes took place when the Earth entered a certain stage of densification. The density of matter inhibits a part of the reproductive force, and the portion still active requires an external complement via the opposite force of another human being. The soul, however, must retain a part of its earlier energy within, both in the man and in the woman. It cannot use this portion in the physical outer world. The retained portion of energy is then directed toward the inner human being. It cannot move toward the exterior and is freed, therefore, for inner organs.

Now appears an important point in human development. Previously what is called spirit—the faculty of thought—could not find a place within the human being, since it could find no organs to accomplish its functions. The soul had employed all its energy toward the exterior, to build up the body. Now, however, the soul's energy that finds no outer use can associate with spiritual energy; and through this, organs are developed in the body that later make the human a thinking being. Thus human beings can use a portion of the energy previously employed for reproduction to perfect their own nature. The force by which the human being forms a thinking brain for itself is the same used to impregnate itself during ancient times. Being single-sexed is the price of thought. By impregnating each other (and no longer impregnating themselves) human beings can turn a part of their reproductive energy inward, and thus become thinking creatures. Consequently, the male body and the female body each represent an imperfect external embodiment of the soul; but in this way human beings become more perfected creatures inwardly.

This transformation of human beings takes place very slowly and gradually. Little by little, the younger, single-sexed male or female forms appear beside the old double-sexed ones.

Again, a kind of fertilization takes place in the human being when it becomes a creature endowed with spirit. The inner organs are built up by the surplus soul energy and are fructified by the spirit. The soul itself is two-sided (male and female), and during ancient times it formed its body on this basis. Later, it could form its external body only by acting together with another body, but thereby the soul itself received the capacity to act together with the spirit. After that the human being fertilized the external from the outside and the internal from the inside, through the spirit.

One could say that the male body now has a female soul, the female body a male soul. This inner one-sidedness of the human being is compensated by fertilization through the spirit, which abolishes the one-sidedness. Both the male soul with its female body and the female soul with its male body become double-sexed again through fructification by the spirit. Thus, men and women are different outwardly; internally their spiritual one-sidedness is rounded out to a harmonious whole. Internally, spirit and soul are fused into a unit. The spirit's effect on the male soul in woman is female, rendering it both male and female; the spirit's effect on the female soul in man is male, making it, too, male and female. The double-sexedness of human beings has retired within from the outer world, where it existed in the pre-Lemurian period.

One can see that the higher inner essence of a human being has nothing to do with man or woman. The inner equality, however, does result from a male soul in woman and from a female soul in man. The union with the spirit finally brings about the equality; but the fact that a difference exists before the establishment of this equality involves a *secret* of human nature. Understanding this secret is of great significance for all mystery science and is the key to important enigmas of life. *For the present we are not permitted to lift the veil spread over this secret....*

Thus the physical human being has developed from a double-sexed to a single-sexed condition, to the separation into male and female. In this way human beings have become spiritual beings of the kind they are now. But we must not assume that beings possessing cognition had not been in contact with the Earth before that time. Indeed, when one follows the Akashic Chronicle, during the first Lemurian period it appears that, because of their double sex, what later became physical human beings were not at all the same as what we call human today. They could not connect sensory perceptions with thoughts and did not think. Impulses constituted their lives, and the soul expressed itself only through instincts, appetites, animal desires, and so on. Their consciousness was dreamlike and lived in dullness.

But there were other beings among these human beings. These of course were also double-sexed, for at that stage of earthly development no male or female human body could be produced; the external conditions did not yet exist. But there were other beings that could acquire knowledge and wisdom in spite of being double-sexed. This was possible because they had gone through a quite different development in a still more remote past. It was possible for their soul to be fructified by the spirit without awaiting the development of the inner organs of the human physical body. With the physical brain, the soul of a contemporary human being can think only what is received from the outside through the physical senses. The development of the human soul has led to this condition. The human soul had to wait until a brain existed to mediate with the spirit. Without this detour, *this* soul would have remained spiritless. It would have remained arrested at the stage of dreamlike consciousness. The situation was different for the superhuman beings mentioned above. In previous stages their soul had developed organs that needed nothing physical to be in contact with the spirit. Their knowledge and wisdom were *supersensibly* acquired. Such knowledge is called *intuitive*. Contemporary human beings will not attain such intuition until they reach a later stage of development. Such intuition will allow human beings to contact the spirit without the mediation of the senses. Meanwhile, human beings must detour through the world of sensory substance; the detour is called the descent of the human soul into matter, or more popularly, the Fall.

Because of a different earlier development, the superhuman beings did not have to take part in this descent. Since their soul had already attained a higher stage, their consciousness was not dreamlike, but inwardly clear. Their acquisition of knowledge and wisdom was a *clairvoyance* having no need of senses or of an organ of thought. The wisdom according to which the world is built shone directly into their soul. Therefore they could become the leaders of youthful humanity, which was still sunk in dullness. They were the bearers of a "primeval wisdom," an understanding human beings are now only struggling toward along the "detour" mentioned. Those beings differed from what we call humankind; wisdom shone upon them as does the sunlight upon us—as a free gift "from above." Human beings were in a different position; they had to acquire wisdom through efforts of the senses and through the organ of thought. It did not come to them originally as a free gift. They had to *desire* it. Human beings acquired it through their senses and the organ of thought only when the *desire* for wisdom lived in them. Thus a new impulse had to awaken in the soul: the desire, the *longing for knowledge*. In its earlier stages the human soul could not have had this longing. The impulses of the soul were directed only toward materialization in what assumed form externally—in what took place in it as a dreamlike life—but not toward cognition of the external world, nor toward knowledge. It is with the division into sexes that the impulse toward knowledge first appears.

The superhuman beings received wisdom by clairvoyance precisely because they did not have the desire for it. They waited until wisdom shone into them, as we wait for the sunlight, which we cannot produce at night, but which must come to us by itself in the morning.

The longing for knowledge is produced as the soul develops inner organs (the brain, and so on), through which it gains knowledge. This happens because part of the soul's energy is directed inwardly instead of outwardly. The superhuman beings have not carried out this separation of their spiritual forces and direct all their soul energy toward the outside. Consequently, they also have available externally for fructification by the spirit the force that human beings turn inward to develop the organs of cognition.

Now that force by which one human being turns toward the outside in order to act together with *another* is *love.* The superhuman beings directed all their *love* outward in order to let universal wisdom flow into their soul. Humankind, however, can direct only a part of it outward. Human beings became sensual, and thereby their love became sensual. They draw away from the outside world that part of their nature they direct toward their inner development. And thus what we call *selfishness* arises. When they became man or woman in the physical body, human beings could surrender themselves with only a part of their being; with the other part they separated themselves from the world around them. They became selfish. And their action toward the outside became selfish; their striving after inner development also became selfish. They loved because they *desired,* and likewise they thought because they *desired* wisdom.

The selfless, all-loving natures, the leaders, the superhuman beings, confronted humanity, which was still selfish in a childish way. The soul of these beings is itself male and female and does not reside in a male or female body. It loves without *desire.* The innocent human soul loved without desire before the division into sexes, but at that time it could not *understand* because it was still at an inferior stage, that of dream consciousness. However, the soul of the superhuman beings, because of its advanced development, loves in this manner with *understanding.* Humanity must pass through selfishness in order to attain *selflessness* again at a higher stage, where, however, it will be combined with completely clear consciousness.

The task of the superhuman natures, of the great leaders, was that they impressed upon youthful humankind their own character, that of *love.* They could do this only for that part of the spiritual energy that was directed outward. Thus, *sensual* love was produced. Sensual love is thus a consequence of the activity of the soul in a male or female body. It became the force of physical human development. This love brings man and woman together insofar as they are physical beings, and upon it rests the progress of physical humanity.

The superhuman natures had power only over this love. Withdrawn from the power of *those* superhuman beings is the part of human soul energy that is inward-directed and is to bring about cognition by the detour through the senses. Those beings had never descended to the development of corresponding inner organs. They could clothe the impulse toward the external in love, because love acting toward the external was part of their own nature. Because of this, a gulf opened between them and youthful humankind. They could plant love, at first in sensual form, in humankind, but they could not give knowledge, for their own knowledge had never made the detour through the inner organs humans were now developing. They could speak no language that a creature with a brain could have understood.

The human inner organs mentioned above first became ripe for contact with the spirit only at the stage of earthly existence lying in the middle of the Lemurian period, but they had already been formed, incompletely, at a much earlier stage of development. For the soul had already gone through physical embodiments in preceding times. It had lived in dense substance, not on Earth but on other celestial bodies. Details about this must be given later. For now, we will say only that the earthly beings previously lived on another planet, where, in accordance with the prevailing conditions, they developed up to the point at which they arrived on Earth. They put off the substances of this preceding planet like clothing and, at the level of development they had attained, became pure soul germs with the capacity to perceive, to feel, and so forth—in short, to lead the dreamlike life that remained peculiar to them in the first stages of their earthly existence.

The superhuman entities previously mentioned, the leaders in the field of love, had already been so perfect on the preceding planet that they did not have to descend to develop the rudiments of those inner organs.

But there were other beings, not as far advanced as these leaders of love, who on the preceding planet were still numbered among "human beings," but at that period were hurrying ahead of human beings. Thus, at the beginning of the formation of the

Earth, they were further advanced than humans, but still were at the stage where knowledge must be acquired through inner organs. These beings were in a special position. They were too far advanced to pass through the physical human body, male or female, but were not so far advanced that they could act through full clairvoyance like the leaders of love. They could not yet be *beings of love;* they could no longer be "human beings." Thus they could continue their own development only as partial superhuman beings, in which they were aided by humans. They could speak to creatures with a brain in a language the latter could understand. Thereby the human soul energy that was turned inward was stimulated, and could connect itself with knowledge and wisdom. It was thus that wisdom of a human kind first appeared on Earth. The "half superhuman beings" could use this human wisdom to achieve for themselves what they still lacked of perfection. In this manner they became the stimulators of human wisdom. One therefore calls them *bringers of light* (Lucifer). Youthful humankind thus had two kinds of leaders: beings of love and beings of wisdom. Human nature was balanced between love and wisdom when it assumed its present form on this Earth. By the beings of love it was stimulated to physical development, by the beings of wisdom to the perfection of the *inner* nature. Through physical development, humanity advances from generation to generation, forms new tribes and races; through inner development, individuals grow toward inner perfection, become knowing and wise people, artists, technicians, and so on. Physical humankind strides from race to race; each race hands down its sensibly perceptible qualities to the following one through physical development. Here the law of heredity holds sway. The children carry within themselves the physical characteristics of their parents. Beyond this, there is a process of spiritual-soul perfection that can occur only through developing the soul itself.

Thus, we stand before the law of the soul's development within earthly existence. This development is related to the law and mystery of *birth* and *death.*

2.
Lucifer and Christ

from *The Christian Mystery*

Lucifer the Bearer of Light, Christ the Bringer of Love

MARCH 30, 1906, DÜSSELDORF

WITHIN the religious confessions of various peoples there is an awareness of two opposing powers; this is also recognized by us in Christianity. The question we will address today concerns these two opposing forces. There are, in fact, powers that we may characterize neither as absolutely good nor as absolutely bad. A power that is good in some connections may be evil in other situations. Think of the natural phenomenon of fire. We must be grateful for fire because of the endless ways it helps us; a new epoch in nature and culture began with the discovery of fire. But fire can also be responsible for evil effects. Schiller described this beautifully in his poem "The Lay of the Bell":

> What friend is like the might of fire,
> When man can watch and wield its ire?
> Whate'er we shape our work, we owe
> Still to that heaven-descended glow,
> When from their chain its wild wings go,
> When where it sitteth, wide and wild
> Sweeps from free Nature's free-born Child.
>
> (*trans., Sir Edward Bulwer-Lytton*)

On the one hand fire is a beneficent power and, on the other, it brings ruin.

Those who look more deeply into life will no longer judge anything as "good" or "evil" under all circumstances. In Christianity the snake or serpent is characterized as the seducer of humankind and, with disgust, called "Lucifer." The view of the luciferic principle has, of course, changed, but Goethe was right in describing the worldview of the average Christian as follows:

> Nature and mind—to Christians we don't speak so,
> Thence to burn atheists we seek so,
> For such discourses very dangerous be.
> Nature is sin and mind is devil:
> Doubt they beget in shameless revel,
> Their hybrid in deformity.
>
> (*trans., Bayard Taylor*)

This was not a view held by primitive Christianity; it entered Christianity only later. Even among the Christian mystics of the first centuries, the Gnostics, the serpent was not a symbol of evil, but rather of the spiritual guidance of humankind. The "wise one," or leader, was called the "serpent." This was the characterization of the one who led human beings to knowledge. The serpent is the symbol for Lucifer.

In the changing Faust legend, we can follow the development of how the Lucifer principle was understood. Faust was a figure from the Middle Ages—half charlatan, half black magician—who practiced all kinds of arts; but he gradually came to represent a certain archetype or symbol to the people of that era. The Faust legend is exactly the opposite of the Luther legend. Luther is the man of God who, with Bible in hand, resists evil and throws an ink bottle at the Devil. Faust, on the other hand, at first sets the Bible aside and becomes a physician, seeking wisdom in place of mere revelations of faith. Faust is fetched by the Devil and is destroyed. Goethe's greatness is that he allows Faust to be redeemed; it is a complete transformation of how the Faust character had been understood in past centuries. Goethe placed the luciferic principle in the form of Mephistopheles over and against Faust. *Mephis* means "liar," *tophel* means "ruiner"; it is a Hebraic name taken from ancient teachings of magic. Faust is the white magician in contrast to Mephistopheles, who represents the emergence of black magic. Goethe does not let Faust fall to Mephistopheles.

The name *Lucifer* means the "bearer of light," from the Latin *lux,* meaning "light," and *fero,* meaning "I bear." This cannot be a principle of evil. To truly understand this principle, we must imagine ourselves back to very ancient times. In order to understand the principle of Lucifer, we must think of the divine and human principles as they were constituted in the earliest times of Christianity. When human beings began to develop, there were other, lower beings, and others that were higher. The higher beings were gods; they had become gods only after a long period of development. These higher beings no longer needed to receive the same teachings human beings need. We think of earthly existence as having been preceded by another planetary existence, during which the gods, who later became creative powers, evolved. The gods have developed ahead of us. In a sense they have already graduated from the school we are now attending. At a certain stage at the outset of their evolution the gods were also human beings.

We need to look at how the various stages of existence are related to one another, beginning with the mineral, plant, and animal kingdoms. When we consider the mineral kingdom we must ask ourselves how it actually arose, a question that leads us to a deep spiritual truth. Take the example of coal, which today is stone. Several million years ago in Earth's evolution, what we heat our stoves with today was still contained in a beautiful forest of ferns. Through a geological catastrophe, the trees were buried and underwent a process that gradually transformed them into coal. Coal confirms the fact that lifeless matter has arisen out of the living. There are constituents of the mineral kingdom for which this is not as easy to ascertain, for example, diamonds and quartz crystals. But these, too, once were a part of life-bearing beings.

If we go further back in time, we find plants that were later petrified into these other minerals. All dead matter has come forth from a single life. If all life were one day to be petrified, the Earth would become a rigid body. Our plants of today are entities that have managed to preserve life from an earlier age, when it was universal. Part became petrified, but another part succeeded in maintaining life. The ancient forests of ferns became petrified; a new kingdom arose, upon which new life then walked. At first there was an age in which there was only life; then came a new age in which part became petrified and a young plant kingdom arose beside it. The mineral kingdom is not chaotic, but rather beautifully organized; there is wisdom in it. The entire framework of the Earth is construed with wisdom. The plant kingdom preserved life, but we can trace life itself back to an even higher kingdom. We can think of all living things as having come forth from this higher kingdom. It is the kingdom of love.

A primal being must have existed there, a being that sheltered love within it. From that being, the kingdom of life separated itself off, and from this kingdom of life the kingdom of wisdom separated off. Besides this, a younger kingdom of love was split off from the original kingdom of love. The beings of this younger kingdom stand at the level of the animal, and already express love for the first time. But there is something still higher. The Divine stands above all these kingdoms. The other kingdoms have all been formed from the Divine. Now you understand how, at the beginning of our planetary evolution, the human being and God faced each other just as the mineral and plant kingdoms of nature stood in relation to each other at the beginning.

Earlier there was a plant kingdom that did not need a mineral kingdom, but the younger plant kingdom needs a mineral kingdom. So, too, at the beginning of Earth's evolution the gods needed humanity. Without human beings the gods could no more have flourished than could the plants without minerals. Consider the animal and the plant kingdoms: there is a very specific relationship between them. The animal exhales carbon dioxide, and the plant exhales oxygen; they are dependent on each other. The lower kingdom, the plant, lovingly gives back to the animal what it needs; the plant keeps the carbon dioxide for itself and gives back the oxygen. Thus we have an ongoing wonderful exchange between lower and higher kingdoms. Such an exchange also exists between the plant and the mineral kingdoms. The plant is constantly lifting the substances of the Earth out of the mineral kingdom and thereby raising them into a life process. In this way a higher kingdom works on a lower kingdom.

Likewise, at the beginning of Earth evolution, the kingdom of the gods worked with the human kingdom. At first there was an interaction like that between plant and mineral, between animal and plant. The interaction between gods and human beings first found expression in what we call love among human beings. When human beings first appeared on the Earth, they embodied both sexes in one organism. This power of love, of relationships between people, is what the Divine used to express itself at the beginning of Earth evolution. The gods receive the love that pulses through human beings and live from it, just as animals live from the oxygen provided by plants. The love that lives in the human race is the nourishment of the gods. In the beginning everything was built on this love. Blood ties connected people; tribes, groups, and peoples were based on it. At the outset of human evolution all the power of the gods was based on this love, which weaves between the sexes.

Before the two sexes came into existence, love existed as a completely conscious love. When human beings became either male or female, the consciousness of love was darkened. It became a blind drive, a sensuality that is not filled with transparent clarity but rather is lived out as a dark force. The gods above reigned in the consciousness of love, but human beings below practiced love as a blind instinct. The gods were nourished by this blind instinct of human love, which for them became a bright light. A clairvoyance is possible that allows everything that lives in the human being as blind instinct to become perceptible. The gods had this vision at the beginning of human evolution, but human beings lacked it. They were filled with passions, flooded with what drives the two sexes together. The gods, who lived in the astral light, saw these drives and lived from them.

Just as earlier a younger plant kingdom remained behind and pushed back the mineral kingdom, so too a new realm of gods arose from an ancient realm of gods; humankind as it is presently constituted then came into existence. There were also beings that had not developed full consciousness in the astral light. They stood between gods and human beings when humanity began its existence on the Earth. We call these beings the hosts of Lucifer. Under the influence of the gods alone, who had attained their perfection during earlier evolution, human beings would have remained without the astral light, without knowledge. These gods were interested in nothing more than that human beings live on the Earth. But Lucifer had to make up for development he had neglected earlier. He could do this only if he employed human beings for this purpose. The realm of the senses was a part of the human kingdom. Lucifer had no sensory existence and had to use the bodies of human beings in order to advance himself. Therefore he had to give human beings the ability to see in the light what the gods had implanted in them. The gods had implanted love in human beings; Lucifer had to seduce them into seeing it in the light. We have then the human being, the shaped form, wisdom. We also have Lucifer, who gives light to humankind, and, finally, God, who floods people with love.

Human Being—Wisdom
Lucifer—Light
God—Love

Lucifer has a much more intimate relationship with human beings than do the gods that reign in love. Lucifer opened the eyes of human beings. When we open our eyes and look out into the world, Lucifer is within us looking out into the world. He is completing his development in us. As long as we were carried in the womb of the gods, we were children of God. Inasmuch as we strive for wisdom, we are friends of Lucifer. This is expressed in the legend of Paradise. Jehovah formed the human being; he is the spirit of form. He would have created human beings so that they live in love without light. Then Lucifer, the snake, came and brought us the light of knowledge and thereby also the possibility of doing evil. Thereupon Jehovah said to the human being that love that is united with the knowledge of Lucifer will bring pain. Jehovah curbed the deeds of the one who implanted love—who brought light to love—by adding pain to love.

In Cain we see the example of one who rebelled against what is created by love bound to the blood. He cut through the blood ties. However, he also represented independence. Alongside passive love is the active, light-filled work of knowledge. Love is a gift from Jehovah, knowledge a gift from Lucifer. Love must be ordered. The organization of familial bonds is derived from the law given on Mount Sinai. Beside it stands knowledge. The origin of the light that should shine from human beings themselves is the light bearer within them. This too, must be deepened; it must experience a new phase, which cannot happen if the law alone holds sway over human beings from the outside. The law works through external compulsion. What Christ brought to the Earth works from inside. It is the light that has been elevated to love, the law that is born in the soul itself. Paul called it grace, the law that is both light and love, which was given from the inside of nature and began a new evolution on Earth. Paul called Christ the new Adam.

The God of love worked above human beings; Lucifer, the light, worked within them. To reach love one must first become light. Through the appearance of Christ Jesus, this light has been transformed into love. Christ Jesus represents the elevation of light to love. In earlier times people spoke of

Lucifer as the opposite pole that brought light to humankind. Two powers must work on the Earth: the bearer of love, or Christ, and the bearer of light, or Lucifer. Light and love are the two poles for humanity. We now live subject to the influences of these two forces that appear as a polarity. The gods who give the impulse for love were once light, and light is now called upon to become love. Light can be misused and lead to evil, but it must exist if we are to become free.

The first Christians saw in Lucifer a force that should work in human nature. This attitude was changed only at a later date. Only someone who has passed through the torture of doubt can be fortified in knowledge. In early Christian times, humankind still had to be protected from the light, but the time has come today when the bond between love and wisdom must once again be created. It is created when knowledge as wisdom is born in human hearts through love. This knowledge born in human hearts through elevation to love is spiritual science.

In ancient times we had the law. Through Christ the law has become grace by having been lifted out of the human being's own heart. Now knowledge can be lifted up again to love. Inward Christianity should be added to the external organization of Christianity. Until now Christianity has been able to realize love only in its institutions, but we must carry love in the greatest depths of the human breast. Today all people still love their own opinions. Love stands above opinions only when people can get along despite the most diverse beliefs. With love above all, the greatest variety of convictions can exist side by side. Then individual opinions do not work alone, but rather all work together in a great choir.

* * *

The Children of Lucifer

From Familial Love to Spiritual Love

APRIL 4, 1906, DÜSSELDORF

It could be said that there are two kinds of people on Earth. Two mighty spiritual streams can be recognized in humanity. One stream strives more to see everything in the light of knowledge, and the other in a certain sense would like to be led. Precisely the way that the spiritual scientific worldview is received shows that striving for bright, clear light is not very widespread. Most people are not yet so far advanced that they want to know something about everything. Many find a certain confusion comforting and are a little embarrassed should they happen to become entirely clear about anything. Actually, however, we must forget everything that can lead to confusion in our consciousness. We must avoid everything that darkens our consciousness, such as alcohol. There are countless other things that lead us away from clarity. Renunciation of these things also makes people more practical in daily life. Faith in authorities also leads to a darkening of consciousness. We should allow ourselves only to be stimulated by authority; we should not build upon it.

What we understand here by the word *clarity* is not related to any subordinate way of seeing into higher worlds. Indeed, such a subordinate approach is connected with a dimming of consciousness in the soul. Mental states of this sort were prevalent in earlier times of human history. During the age of the Atlanteans, human consciousness was much less clear than now. Even the most primitive peoples today are advanced far beyond the state of consciousness attained by the Atlanteans. As we go back further and further in the evolution of humankind, we come increasingly to states in which human beings see from within but do not understand with the intellect. The intellect began to be just barely perceptible with the Atlantean race.

At a certain time the Atlanteans lived in a place that included present-day Ireland. When Atlanteans approached one another, astral pictures arose in their consciousness. They could not yet reflect. Only after the frontal lobe of the brain was developed could human beings say "I" of themselves. Human beings first started to develop their I-consciousness in that part of Atlantis that is Ireland today. From this location the Atlanteans spread over Europe toward Asia. The human evident in the skeletal remains known as Neanderthal derived from descendants of Atlanteans having a sloped forehead. From that time on, we very slowly learned to think with our minds and develop I-consciousness.

When human beings began their existence fructified by the spirit here on the Earth, they were far beyond the animals but could not yet speak or think. Spiritual beings called *devas* were present at that time. They needed no physical body; they had floated in astral space on Old Moon and had already acquired what they could achieve with a physical body. There were also other beings who had not concluded their evolution on the Moon, who were not finished with their Moon evolution. These were luciferic beings who, compared with the *devas*, had remained behind in their development. The gods, or *devas*, lived from what had become a characteristic of human beings on the Earth, from love between the sexes. Human love is the air or the nourishment enjoyed by the gods. In Greek mythology it was characterized as nectar and ambrosia.

As long as human beings slept, the hosts of Lucifer had no proper role in humankind. They made human beings into their own children only during the fifth root race. Human thinking is not really very old. What is called ancient primeval wisdom was native to the most ancient peoples. This primeval wisdom is ancient priestly wisdom that was revealed from within. Knowing proper actually arose only a few centuries before Christ's birth, about 600 B.C. The power of judgment was also developed only later.

We come to an important mystery with a phenomenon that we find among ancient peoples. Only someone who casts light into the soul world is in a position to understand this phenomenon. Among North American Indian tribes we find unusual names for familial relationships. The children of siblings were called "siblings" among the Iroquois, but only the children of brothers, not those of sisters. This is a residue of ancient Atlantis. During the earliest ages of the history of humankind the familial connection was the only one that counted. The women had several husbands, and it was not possible to specify who the children's fathers were. All peoples had ancestors who were not so intent upon not marrying close relatives. A close blood tie was not a hindrance to marriage. It was said that children produced by parents who were next of kin were the most highly illuminated: they were somnambulistic.

Now further evolution leads ever more to the conditions where marriages take place between people who are not related. There is a law that the union of unrelated people loosens the etheric body from the physical body. Marriage of blood relatives caused the etheric body of descendants to sit firmly in the physical. They were illuminated from within. They thought more with their solar plexus, but they had no judgment. Judgment grows with marriage of unrelated people and appears to the extent that ancient blood-relative marriages recede. The old somnambulistic clairvoyance then disappears, and a new kind of seeing appears, the power of judgment. This new epoch is characterized by the rise of the Dionysian principle. Dionysos was torn apart; only his heart was saved. When the Dionysian impulse appeared, human beings were torn apart and then put back together again by the heart, the relationship in the soul that is connected with a complete change of the sexual life. The intellect is a transformation of what earlier was sexuality among relatives.

Humanity's early stages of development are now repeated in seven-year rhythms in individual human lives. From birth to the seventh year, the etheric body of the child is still completely in the background. For this reason, before the seventh year the child's memory should not yet be trained, but rather only the senses. We can develop the senses and hence awaken inner forces with the help of the senses. These forces should be stimulated by giving children toys that allow fantasy to be active, for example, wooden blocks with dots painted on for eyes and so on, but no finished dolls that allow nothing more to be added by fantasy.

From the seventh to the fourteenth years, children must be trained with firm habits that will give them a certain solidity in later life. During these years everything concerned with the development of the memory should be brought to the fore. Therefore it is better if we do not attempt to develop the powers of judgment during this stage. Children should be surrounded by authority but not be authorities themselves. We should influence the children with stories, not with moralizing sermons. They need to hear of great examples and models. To teach morals it would be necessary to develop feelings for them in the ancient Pythagorean ways. Pythagoras told his disciples they should not swing their swords at a fire, illustrating that you should not do useless things. Another Pythagorean expression was that you should not reverse your path until you have come to its end. Children should not be taught to judge things themselves until after puberty. At that age the etheric body is loosened, and the astral body is only just ready to be active outwardly.

The development that individual human beings now pass through in seven-year rhythms was completed by humankind in the course of its enormous evolutionary epochs. Part of the human being's inferior powers were elevated to be formed into the power of judgment. Only then could the hosts of Lucifer intervene. This luciferic power is expressed in independent human judgment. At the time of this luciferic intervention, work accomplished by human beings appeared for the first time. If we follow this development in ancient times, we can say that at that time only families joined together in community. Those who wanted to establish the purely spiritual in place of blood relationships were those working in the name of Lucifer.

The Church was formed as a continuation of the ancient wisdom of the priests. Alongside it arose a stream that sought light itself, the luciferic people such as the Knights Templar. They said that one must seek light and truth for oneself. There was a sect in the Middle Ages that understood this. Its members called themselves "Luciferians."[1] They said that no matter how blessed human beings could become without the light of knowledge, they were not interested; they wanted to penetrate to the light. These are the two streams in humanity. One stream wants only

1. *Luciferians* were followers of Bishop Lucifer Calaritanus of Cagliari (d. 370). Bishop Lucifer was vehemently opposed to Arianism. He defended Athanasius at the council of Milan, and was exiled by Emperor Constantius II in 355. For a time there were Luciferians in Sardinia, Spain, Gaul, Italy, and Africa.

to become blessed, and the other also wants light. Those afraid of knowledge consider Lucifer to be the evil one, but for the others Lucifer is the light bringer, the light bearer. There is a manuscript in the Vatican that speaks of this, but it is kept secret by the Church; this ecclesiastical attitude warns people of Lucifer. The dogma of the Church can certainly contain truth. In this sense a Pythagorean axiom can be a dogma for those who do not understand it, but when it is understood, it becomes bright, clear knowledge. Dogmas are presented as founded on authority. When we understand them, they become clear knowledge.

At the time when Paul lived, Christianity was supposed to lead to universal human love. A world religion was to arise from a tribal folk religion. Faith in revelation was dependent on a community based on blood. Moses gave firm laws. Christ did not impart set laws; in place of the law we find grace, the awakening of the innermost part of the human soul. The organization of the Church strove for something that represents a descending wave, while the striving for freedom of opinion represents an ascending wave. Such striving existed in certain brotherhoods, for example among the Knights Templar, who strive for the light. This group that strives for the light represents the children of Lucifer.

Edouard Schuré sets his drama *The Children of Lucifer* during the time when Christianity began to be strictly organized.[2] There is an ecclesiastical stream and next to it the other, the luciferic principle. The children of Lucifer are the children of the inner light, not of faith in revelation. Those who strive toward the future must feel themselves related. That one should

2. See Rudolf Steiner & Edouard Schuré, *The East in the Light of the West / Children of Lucifer*, Spiritual Science Library, Blauvelt, NY, 1986.

come to the light through one's own striving is expressed in our time through the spiritual scientific movement. A deeply rooted inner freedom should be developed within the human soul.

The theosophical periodical is intentionally named *Lucifer.*[3] The name is connected with the inner essence of the theosophical movement. It should be documented that the luciferic principle was once consciously thrown into the world. At the time when the Catholic Church asserted the dogma of infallibility, the luciferic principles appeared as an opposite-striving pole. One could say that theosophy's proclaiming of spiritual freedom brought about as a counterpole the dogma of infallibility, which is the only way the Catholic Church could save itself.

3. Material published in *Luzifer* and in *Lucifer-Gnosis* is available in German in *Lucifer-Gnosis: Grundlegende Aufsätze zur Anthroposophie und Berichte aus "Luzifer" und "Lucifer-Gnosis" 1903-1908,* Rudolf Steiner Gesamtausgabe, Dornach, Switzerland, 1987.

3.
THE MISSION OF REVERENCE

OCTOBER 28, 1909, BERLIN

from *Metamorphoses of the Soul*

YOU are all familiar with Goethe's words that conclude his life's masterpiece *Faust*:

> All things transient
> Are but a parable;
> Earth's insufficiency
> Here finds fulfillment;
> The indescribable
> Here becomes deed;
> The eternal feminine
> Draws us on high.

It goes without saying that, in this context, "eternal feminine" has nothing to do with gender. Goethe is using an ancient figure of speech. In all forms of mysticism—and Goethe gives these closing lines to a *Chorus mysticus*—we find an urge in the soul, at first quite indefinite, toward something it has not yet come to know or to unite itself with, but must strive toward. In accord with mystics of diverse times, Goethe calls this goal, at first only dimly surmised by the aspiring soul, the eternal feminine; the whole sense of the second part of *Faust* confirms this meaning of the concluding lines.

The *Chorus mysticus*, with its succinct words, can be set against the *Unio mystica*, the name true mystical thinkers give to union with the eternal feminine, far off spiritually but within human reach. When the soul has risen to this height and feels itself to be at one with the eternal feminine, then we can speak of mystical union, and it is this summit we will be considering today.

In the previous two lectures, on the mission of anger and the mission of truth, we saw that the soul is involved in a process of evolution.[1] On the one hand, we indicated that the soul must strive to overcome certain attributes, anger for example, which thereby can become educators of the soul; on the other hand, we saw how truth can educate the soul in its own special way.

The end and goal of this process of development cannot always be foreseen by the soul. We can place some object before us and say that it has developed from an earlier form to its present stage, but we cannot say this of the human soul, for the soul is progressing through a continuing evolution where it is itself the active agent. The soul must feel that, having developed to a certain point, it has to go further. And as a self-aware soul it must say to itself: How is it that I am able to think not only about my development in the past but also about my development in the future?

Now we have often explained how the soul, with all its inner life, is composed of three members. We cannot go over this in detail again today, but it will be better to mention it, so that this lecture can be studied on its own account. We call these three members of the soul the Sentient Soul, the Intellectual Soul, and the Consciousness Soul. The Sentient Soul can live without

1. See *Metamorphoses of the Soul: Paths of Experience,* vol. 1, Rudolf Steiner Press, London, 1983.

being much permeated by thinking. Its primary role is to receive impressions from the outer world and to pass them on inwardly. It is also the vehicle of feelings such as pleasure and pain, joy and grief, that come from these outer impressions. All human emotions, all desires, instincts, and passions arise within the Sentient Soul. Humankind has progressed from this stage to higher levels and has permeated the Sentient Soul with thinking and with feelings induced by thinking. In the Intellectual Soul, accordingly, we do not find indefinite feelings arising from the depths, but feelings gradually penetrated by the inner light of thought. At the same time, we find that emerging by degrees from the Intellectual Soul is the human I—the central point of the soul that can lead to the real Self and makes it possible for us to purify, cleanse, and refine the qualities of our soul from within, so that we can become the master, leader, and guide of our volitions, feelings, and thoughts.

This I, as we have seen, has two aspects. One way to develop it is through the endeavors human beings must make to strengthen this inner center more and more, so that an increasingly powerful influence can radiate from it into the environment and all the surrounding life. Enhancing the value of the soul for the surrounding world while strengthening its independence is one aspect of I development.

The reverse side of this is egoism. A Self that is too weak will lose itself in the flood of the world. But if a person likes to keep all pleasures and desires, all thinking and brooding, within, the I will be hardened and given over to self-seeking and egoism.

We have briefly described the content of the Intellectual Soul and have seen that wild impulses, anger for example, can educate the soul if they are overcome and conquered. We have seen also that the Intellectual Soul is positively educated by truth when truth is understood as something we possess inwardly and take account of at all times, when it leads us out of ourselves and enlarges the I while strengthening it and making it more selfless.

Thus we have become acquainted with the means of self-education provided for the Sentient Soul and the Intellectual Soul. Now we have to ask if a similar means is provided for the Consciousness Soul, the highest member of the human soul. We can also ask, What in the Consciousness Soul develops of its own accord, corresponding to the instincts and desires in the Sentient Soul? Is there something that belongs by nature to the Consciousness Soul, such that human beings could acquire very little of it if they were not already endowed with it?

There is something that reaches out from the Intellectual Soul to the Consciousness Soul—the strength and sagacity of thinking. The Consciousness Soul can come to expression only because human beings are thinking beings, for its task is to acquire knowledge of the world and of itself, and for this it requires the highest instrument of knowledge—thinking.

We learn about the external world through perceptions; they stimulate us to gain knowledge of our surroundings. To this end, we need only devote our attention to the outer world and not stand blankly in front of it, for then the outer world itself draws us on to satisfy our thirst for knowledge by observing it. With regard to gaining knowledge of the supersensible world, we are in a quite different situation. First of all, the supersensible world is not there in front of us. If we wish to gain knowledge of it so that this knowledge will permeate our Consciousness Soul, the impulse to do so must come from within and must penetrate our thinking through and through. This impulse can come only from the other powers of the soul, from feeling and willing. Unless our thinking is stimulated by both these powers, it will never be impelled to approach the supersensible world. This does not mean that the supersensible is merely a feeling, but that feeling and willing must act as inner guides toward its unknown realm.

What qualities, then, must feeling and willing acquire in order to do this? First of all, someone might object to the use of a feeling as a guide to knowledge. But a simple consideration will show that in fact this is what feeling does. Anyone who takes knowledge seriously, will admit that in acquiring knowledge we must proceed logically. We use logic as an instrument for testing the knowledge we acquire. How, then, if logic is this instrument, can logic itself be proved? One might say that logic can prove itself. Yes, but before we begin proving logic by logic, it must be at least possible to grasp logic with our feeling. Logical thought cannot be proved primarily by logical thought, but only by feeling. Indeed, everything that constitutes logic is first proved by feeling, by the infallible feeling for truth that dwells in the human soul. From this classic example we can see how feeling is the foundation of logic and of thinking. Feeling must give the impulse for the verification of thought. What must feeling become if it is to provide an impulse not only for thinking in general, but for thinking about worlds we are at first unacquainted with and cannot survey?

Feeling of this kind must be a force that strives from within toward an object yet unknown. When the human soul seeks to encompass some other thing with feeling, we call this feeling love. Love can of course be felt for something known, and there are many things in the world for us to love. But as love is a feeling, and as feeling is the foundation of thinking in the widest sense, we must be clear that the unknown supersensible can be grasped by feeling before thinking comes in. Accordingly, unprejudiced observation shows that it must be possible for human beings to come to love the unknown supersensible before they are able to conceive it in terms of thought. This love is indeed indispensable before the supersensible can be penetrated by the light of thought.

At this stage, also, the will can be permeated by a force that goes out toward the supersensible unknown. This quality of the will that enables human beings to wish to carry out their aims and intentions with regard to the unknown is devotion. So the will can inspire devotion toward the unknown, while feeling becomes love of the unknown; and when these two emotions are united they give rise to reverence in the true sense of the word. Then devotion becomes the impulse that will lead us into the unknown, so that the unknown can be taken hold of by our thinking. Thus it is that reverence becomes the educator of the Consciousness Soul, for in ordinary life, also, we can say that when we endeavor to grasp with our thinking some external reality we do not yet know, we will be approaching it with love and devotion. The Consciousness Soul will never gain a knowledge of external objects unless love and devotion inspire its quest; otherwise the objects will not be truly observed. This also applies quite especially to all endeavors to gain knowledge of the supersensible world

In all cases, however, the soul must allow itself to be educated by the I, the source of self-awareness. We have seen how the I gains increasing independence and strength by overcoming certain soul qualities, such as anger, and by cultivating others, such as the sense of truth. After that, the self-education of the I comes to an end; its education through reverence begins. Anger is to be overcome and discarded; a sense of truth is to permeate the I; reverence is to flow from the I toward the object one seeks to know. Thus, having raised itself out of the Sentient Soul and the Intellectual Soul by overcoming anger and other passions and by cultivating a sense of truth, the I is drawn gradually into the Consciousness Soul by the influence of reverence. If this reverence becomes stronger and stronger, one can speak of it as a powerful impulse toward the realm described by Goethe:

All things transient
Are but a parable;
Earth's insufficiency
Here finds fulfillment;
The indescribable
Here becomes deed;
The eternal feminine
Draws us on high.

The soul is drawn by the strength of its reverence toward the eternal, with which it longs to unite. But the I has two sides. It is impelled by necessity to enhance continually its own strength and activity. At the same time it has the task of not allowing itself to fall under the hardening influence of egoism. If the I seeks to go further and gain knowledge of the unknown and the supersensible, and takes reverence as its guide, it is exposed to the immediate danger of losing itself. This, above all, is most likely to happen to a human being whose will is always submissive to the world. If this attitude increasingly gains the upper hand, the I may go out of itself and lose itself in the other being or thing it has submitted to. This condition can be likened to the soul fainting, as distinct from bodily fainting. When the body faints, the I sinks into undefined darkness; when the soul faints, the I loses itself spiritually while the bodily faculties and perceptions of the outer world are not impaired. This can happen if the I is not strong enough to extend itself fully into the will and to guide it.

This self-surrender by the I can be the final result of a systematic mortification of the will. Those who pursue this course become incapable of willing or acting on their own account; they have surrendered their will to the object of their submissive devotion and have lost their own Self. When this condition prevails, it produces an enduring impotence of the soul. Only when a devotional feeling is warmed through by the I, so that one can be immersed in it without losing the I, can it be salutary for the human soul.

How, then, can reverence always carry the I with it? The I, as a human Self, cannot allow itself to be led in any direction unless it maintains in its thinking a knowledge of itself. Nothing else can protect the I from losing itself when devotion leads it out into the world. The soul can be led by the force of will out of itself toward something external, but when it goes beyond the limits of the external, it must be sure it is illuminated by the light of thought.

Thinking itself cannot lead the soul out; this comes about through devotion, but thinking must then immediately exert itself to permeate the object of the soul's devotion with the life of thought. In other words, there must be a resolve to think about this object. As soon as the devotional impulse loses the will to think, there is a danger of losing the Self. Making it a matter of principle not to think about the object of one's devotion can lead in extreme cases to a lasting debility of the soul.

Is love, the other element in reverence, exposed to a similar fate? Something that radiates from the human Self toward the unknown must be poured into love, so that never for a moment does the I fail to sustain itself. The I must have the will to enter everything that forms the object of its devotion, and it must maintain itself in the face of the external, the unknown, the supersensible. What becomes of love if the I fails to maintain itself at the moment of encountering the unknown, if it is unwilling to bring the light of thinking and of rational judgment to bear on the unknown? Love of that kind becomes more sentimental enthusiasm (*Schwarmerei*). But the I can begin to find its way from the Intellectual Soul, where it lives, to the external unknown, and there it can never extinguish itself altogether. Unlike the will, the I cannot completely mortify itself. When the soul seeks to embrace the external world with feeling, the I is always present in the feeling, but if it is not supported by thinking and willing, it rushes forth without restraint, unconscious of itself. And if this love for the unknown is not accompanied by resolute thinking, the soul can fall into a sentimental extreme, somewhat like sleepwalking, just as the state reached by the soul when submissive devotion leads to loss of the Self is somewhat like the body fainting. When sentimental enthusiasts go forth to encounter the unknown, they leave behind the strength of the I and take along only secondary forces. Since the strength of the I is absent from their consciousness, they try to grasp the unknown as one does in the realm of dreams. Under these conditions the soul falls into what may be called an enduring state of dreaming or somnambulism.

Again, if the soul is unable to relate itself properly to the world and to other people, if it rushes out into life and shrinks from using the light of thought to illuminate its situation, then the I falls into a somnambulistic condition and is bound to go astray and to wander through the world like a will-o'-the-wisp.

Only the soul that succumbs to mental laziness and shuns the light of thought when it meets the unknown will harbor superstitions in one form or other. The sentimental soul, with its fond dreams, wandering through life as though asleep, and the indolent soul, unwilling to be fully conscious of itself, are the souls most inclined to believe everything blindly. Their tendency is to avoid the effort of thinking for themselves and to allow truth and knowledge to be prescribed for them.

If we are to get to know an external object, we have to bring our own productive thinking to bear on it, and it is the same with the supersensible, whatever form this may take. In seeking to gain knowledge of the supersensible, we must never exclude thinking. As soon as we rely on merely observing the supersensible, we are exposed to all possible deceptions and errors. All such errors and superstitions, all the wrong or untruthful ways of entering the supersensible worlds, can be attributed in the last instance to a refusal to allow consciousness to be illuminated by the light of creative thought. No one who has the will to always think actively and independently can be deceived by information said to come from the spiritual world. Nothing else will suffice, and every spiritual researcher will confirm this. The stronger the will to creative thinking, the greater is the possibility of gaining true, clear, and certain knowledge of the spiritual world.

Thus we see the need for a means of education that will lead the I into the Consciousness Soul and will guide the Consciousness Soul in the face of the unknown, both the physical unknown and the supersensible. Reverence, consisting of devotion and love, provides the means we seek. When devotion and love are imbued with the right kind of self-feeling, they become steps that lead to ever greater heights.

True devotion, in whatever form it is experienced by the soul, whether through prayer or otherwise, can never lead anyone astray. The best way to learn to know something is to approach it first of all with love and devotion. A healthy education will consider especially how strength can be given to the development of the soul through the devotional impulse. The world is largely unknown to children: if we are to guide them toward knowledge and sound judgment of it, the best way is to awaken in them a feeling of reverence toward it. And we can be sure that by so doing we will lead them to fullness of experience in any walk of life.

It is very important for the human soul if it can look back to a childhood when devotion, leading on to reverence, was often felt. Frequent opportunities to look up to revered persons, and to gaze with heartfelt devotion at things that are still beyond its understanding, provide a good impulse for higher development in later life. People will always gratefully remember those occasions when, as children in the family circle, they heard of some outstanding personality whom everyone spoke of with devotion and reverence. A feeling of holy awe, which gives reverence an especially intimate character, will then permeate the soul. Or someone may relate how, later on, he or she rang the bell with trembling hand and shyly entered the room of the revered personality who had been spoken of with so much respectful admiration and was now being met for the first time. Simply to have come into the presence of such a person and exchanged a few words can confirm a devotion that will be particularly helpful when we are trying to unravel the great riddles of existence and are seeking the goal we long to make our own. Here reverence is a force that draws us upward, and by so doing fortifies and invigorates the soul. How can this be? Let us consider the outward expression of reverence in human gestures—what forms does it take? We bend our knees, fold our hands, and incline our heads toward the object of our reverence. These are the organs whereby the I and, above all, the higher faculties of the soul can express themselves most intensively.

In physical life a person stands upright by firmly extending the legs; in acts of blessing, one's I radiates out through the hands; and by moving the head one can observe the earth or the heavens. But from studying human nature, we learn also that our legs are stretched out at their best in strong, conscious action if they have first learned to bend the knee where reverence is really due. For this genuflection opens the door to a force that seeks to find its way into our organism. Knees that have not learned to bend in reverence give out only what they have always had; they spread out their own nullity, to which they have added nothing. But legs that have learned to genuflect receive, when they are extended, a new force, and then this, not their own nullity, is what they spread around them. Hands that would feign to bless and comfort, although they have never been folded in reverence and devotion, cannot bestow much love and blessing from their own nullity. But hands that have learned to fold themselves in reverence have received a new force and are powerfully penetrated by the I, for the path taken by this force leads first through the heart, where it kindles love. And the reverence of the folded hands, having passed through the heart and flowed into the hands, turns into blessing.

The head may turn its eyes and strain its ears to survey the world in all directions, but it presents nothing but its own emptiness. If, however, the head has been bent in reverence, it gains a new force; it will bring the feelings it has acquired through reverence to meet the outer world.

Anyone who studies the gestures of people and knows what they signify will see how reverence is expressed in external physiognomy and how it enhances the strength of the I, making it possible for the I to penetrate into the unknown. Moreover, this self-education through reverence has the effect of raising to the surface our obscure instincts and emotions, our sympathies and antipathies, which otherwise make their way into the soul unconsciously or subconsciously, unchallenged by the light of judgment. Precisely these feelings are cleansed and purified through self-education by reverence and through the penetration by the I of the higher members of the soul. The obscure forces of sympathy and antipathy, always prone to error, are permeated by the light of the soul and transformed into judgment, aesthetic taste, and rightly guided moral feeling. A soul educated by reverence will convert its dark cravings and aversions into a feeling for the beautiful and a feeling for the good. A soul that has cleansed its obscure instincts and will impulses through devotion will gradually build up from them what we call moral ideals. Reverence is something that we plant in the soul as a seed; and the seed will bear fruit.

Human life offers yet another example. We see everywhere that the course of a human life goes through ascending and declining stages. Childhood and youth are stages of ascent; then comes a pause, and finally, in the later years, a decline. Now, the remarkable thing is that the qualities acquired in childhood and youth reappear in a different form during the years of decline. If much reverence, rightly guided, has been part of the experience of childhood, it acts as a seed that comes to fruition in old age as strength for active living. If devotion and love were not fostered under the right guidance during childhood and youth, it leads to a weak and powerless old age. Reverence must take hold of every soul that is to make progress in its development.

How is it, then, with the corresponding quality in the object of our reverence? If we look with love on another being, then the reciprocated love of the latter will reveal what can perhaps arise. If we are lovingly devoted to our God, we can be sure that God inclines to us also in love. Reverence is the feeling we develop for whatever we call God out there in the universe. Since the reaction to reverence cannot itself be called reverence, we may not speak of a divine reverence toward humans. What, then, is precisely the opposite of reverence in this context? What is it that flows out to meet reverence when reverence seeks the Divine? It is might, the almighty power of the Divine. Reverence that we learn to feel in youth returns to us as strength for living in old age, and if we turn in reverence to the Divine, our reverence flows back to us as an experience of the Almighty. That is what we feel, whether we look up to the starry heavens in their endless glory and our reverence goes out to all that lies around us, beyond our compass, or whether we look up to our invisible God, in whatever form, who pervades and animates the cosmos.

We look up toward the Almighty and come to feel with certainty that we cannot advance toward union with what is above us unless we first approach it from below with reverence. We draw nearer to the Almighty when we immerse ourselves in reverence. Thus we can speak of an Almighty in this sense, while a true feeling for the meaning of words prevents us from speaking of an All-loving. Power can be increased or enhanced in proportion to the number of beings over which it extends. It is different with love. If a child is loved by its mother, this does not prevent her from loving equally her second, third, or fourth child. It is false for anyone to say, I must divide up my love because it is to cover two objects. It is false to speak either of an "all-knowledge" or of an indefinite "all-love." Love has no degree and cannot be limited by figures.

Love and devotion together make up reverence. We can have a devoted attitude to this or that unknown if we have the right feeling for it. Devotion can be enhanced, but it does not have to be divided up or multiplied when it is felt for a number of beings. Since this is true also of love, the I has no need to lose or disperse itself if it turns with love and devotion toward the unknown. Love and devotion are thus the right guides to the unknown, and the best educators of the soul in its advance from the Intellectual Soul to the Consciousness Soul.

Whereas overcoming anger educates the Sentient Soul, and striving for truth educates the Intellectual Soul, reverence educates the Consciousness Soul, bringing more and more knowledge within its reach. But this reverence must be led and guided from a standpoint that never shuts out the light of thought. When love flows forth from us, it ensures by its own worth that our Self can go with it, and this applies also to devotion. We could indeed lose our Self, but we need not. That is the point, and it must be kept especially in mind if an impulse of reverence enters the education of the young. A blind, unconscious reverence is never right. Cultivating reverence must go together with cultivating a healthy I-feeling.

Whereas the mystics of all ages, together with Goethe, have spoken of the unknown, undefined element to which the soul is drawn as the eternal feminine, we may without misunderstanding speak of the element that must always animate reverence as the eternal masculine. For just as the eternal feminine is present in both man and woman, so is this eternal masculine, this healthy I-feeling, present in all reverence by man or woman. And when Goethe's *Chorus mysticus* comes before us, we may, having come to know the mission of reverence that leads us toward the unknown, add the element that must permeate all reverence—the eternal masculine.

Thus we are now able to reach a right understanding of the experience of the human soul when it strives to unite itself with the unknown and attains to the *Unio mystica,* wherein all reverence is consummated.

But this mystical union will harm the soul if the I is lost while seeking to unite itself with the unknown in any form. If the I has lost itself, it will bring to the unknown nothing of value. Self-sacrifice in the *Unio mystica* requires that one must have become something, must have something to sacrifice. If a weak I, with no strength in itself, is united with what lies above us, the union has no value. The *Unio mystica* has value only when a strong I ascends to the regions spoken of by the *Chorus mysticus.* Then, when Goethe speaks of the regions to which the higher reverence can lead us in order to gain the highest knowledge, and when his *Chorus mysticus* tells us in the beautiful words:

> All things transient
> Are but a parable;
> Earth's insufficiency
> Here finds fulfillment;
> The indescribable
> Here becomes deed;
> The eternal feminine
> Draws us on high.

If we understand the *Unio mystica* correctly, we can reply: Yes,

All things transient
Are but a parable;
Earth's insufficiency
Here finds fulfillment;
The indescribable
Here becomes deed;
The eternal masculine
Draws us on high.

4.
Love: The Mission of the Earth
I

MAY 20, 1908, HAMBURG

from *The Gospel of St. John*

YESTERDAY we saw what profound contents are concealed within the first words of the Gospel of St. John.[1] We can summarize our observations by saying that the writer of this Gospel pointed to the creation of a pre-humanity in the far distant past and indicated that, according to esoteric Christianity, everything leads back to the Word, or *Logos*. The Logos was a creating power as early as the ancient Saturn period; it then became *Life* while our Earth passed through its existence as the Sun; and while the Earth passed through the ancient Moon state, it became *Light*.[2]

Under the influence of divine spiritual forces and powers, the human creature, over the course of those three planetary states of evolution, reached the point in development of being penetrated by the human I—the Earth having now developed into our present planet. Thus we may say that, like a kind of

1. Lecture of May 19, 1908, "Esoteric Christianity."

2. For a greater understanding of the "planetary" stages of evolution, see *An Outline of Esoteric Science*, "Cosmic Evolution and the Human Being."

seed, a creature passed to the Earth from the ancient Moon and consisted of a physical body derived from the divine, primal Word—an ether or life body whose source was divine Life, and an astral body that issued from divine Light. During that creature's life on the Earth, the light of the I itself was kindled within its inmost being, and this threefold bodily nature—the physical, etheric, and astral—gained the capacity to say to itself, "I AM." In a certain sense we may call Earth evolution the evolution of the "I AM," the evolution of the self-awareness of the human race. This "I AM," this capacity for full self-awareness, developed slowly and gradually in the course of the evolution of human beings on Earth. We must clearly understand how this evolution proceeded, how slowly and gradually the I, full self-awareness, appeared within human beings.

The stage of our earthly evolution that we call the ancient Lemurian period is the earliest period of our life on Earth in which human beings appeared in the form we, in general, possess today. Then, for the first time, what we may call the incarnation of the I, the true inner being of humankind, took place in the three bodies, the astral, ether, and physical bodies. After that came the Atlantean period when humans lived for the most part on the ancient continent of Atlantis, a region that sank beneath the water through the great Atlantean flood and today forms the bed of the Atlantic Ocean. Remembrance of this event has been preserved in the deluge sagas of nearly all peoples. During the post-Atlantean period right up to our present day, human beings have passed through successive incarnations, in harmony with their inner natures. As has been stated, it was during the Lemurian period that our souls were incarnated for the first time in a threefold entity consisting of physical body, ether body, and astral body, as we have learned to know them. What preceded this will be left for a later consideration. Thus we must go far back into the past if we wish to consider the course of evolution, for the human being evolved very slowly and gradually to its present condition of existence.

From the standpoint of spiritual science, what does esotericism call our "present" existence? It calls it a state of consciousness that contemporary human beings possess from the time they awaken in the morning until they fall asleep in the evening. During that time, they see the objects about them by means of their outer physical senses. From the time they fall asleep in the evening until they awaken in the morning, they do not see the objects about them. Why is this so? We know that it is because during the day, under present evolutionary conditions, the real inner human being, namely the I and the astral body, is within the physical and ether bodies on the physical plane; in other words, they are in the physical world. Thus the astral body and the I can make use of the physical organs for hearing and seeing in the physical world, for observing physical things. From the time we fall asleep in the evening until we awaken in the morning, the I and the astral body are out of the physical world on the astral plane. There they are detached from the physical eyes and ears, and therefore are not able to observe what is about them.

The alternating state of being awake by day and asleep by night developed slowly and gradually. This was not yet the case in the ancient Lemurian period when the human being for the first time passed through a physical incarnation. At that time the I and the astral body were within the physical body for only a very brief portion of the day, by no means as long a period as now. Because the human being was outside the physical body for a longer time and entered it only for a brief period in a waking state, life during the Lemurian period was very different from life as we experience it. Our state of unconsciousness during the night, when we are not merely dreaming, is a state that has developed slowly and gradually. Day-consciousness and night-consciousness were very differently apportioned during the Lemurian period. At that time human beings still possessed a dull clairvoyant consciousness, and during the night, when they were out of the physical body and in the spirit world, they perceived this spirit world around them, although not so clearly as we of the present see the physical objects around us during the day. We should not simply compare this perceiving in the spiritual world with the present dreaming. The present dream state is only like a last stunted remnant of this ancient clairvoyance. However, the kind of images perceived then were similar to what we perceive today in dreams, but with a very real meaning. Let us be very clear about the meaning of these images.

In ancient times when human beings lived a very brief portion of the twenty-four hours in waking consciousness, a much shorter time than we do today, they saw external, physical objects very dimly as though wrapped in a mist. The capacity to see physical objects as we do today developed very slowly. At that time they saw the first indication of a physical body enveloped in a mist, just as we see the lamps surrounded by a mist, by a kind of light aura, when we walk through the streets on a misty evening. This, however, is only an illusion, but that is the way humans at first saw physical bodies emerging about them. And when they slept they did not sink into unconsciousness; during their sleep consciousness, images emerged, pictures in color and form, and around them was a world, in comparison with which the most vivid dreamworld of today is only a weak, dim echo. These images signified something psychic and spiritual in their environment. At that time, in the beginning of the earthly course of human beings, when they approached a dangerous creature during their night wanderings, they did not see it as we would see it now—for example, they did not see the approaching lion as a lion's form, but as an emerging image of color and form, which instinctively told them that here was something harmful, something that would devour them, something they must avoid. These were true images of something psycho-spiritual occurring about them. All that belonged to the soul and spirit was seen in the night, and evolution proceeded in such a way that slowly and gradually human beings immersed themselves in the physical body for a longer and longer time. The night grew ever shorter, the day lasted longer and longer; and the more humans lived within the physical body, the more the nightly clairvoyant images disappeared and the more the present waking consciousness emerged.

However, we must not forget that a truly genuine self-awareness, which should be acquired during life upon the Earth, can only be attained by submersion in a physical body. Prior to this, human beings did not feel themselves as independent entities, but as a part of divine spiritual beings from whom they were descended. Still possessing a dull clairvoyance, they felt themselves part of a divine spiritual consciousness, part of a divine I, just as the hand feels itself part of the physical organism. They could not have said of themselves, "I AM," but would have said "God is," and "I in Him."

As we shall see more and more, a very special mission was reserved for the Earth, which during its evolution had passed through three earlier stages, Saturn, Sun, and Moon. Do not imagine that the different planetary life conditions can be considered as existing beside one another, one planet exactly equivalent to the other. Divine creation is not simply a repetition of something already existing. Each planetary existence has a very definite mission. The mission of our Earth is the cultivation of the principle of love to its highest degree by the beings evolving upon it. When the Earth has reached the end of its evolution, love should permeate it through and through. Let us understand clearly what is meant by the expression, "the Earth is the planetary life condition for the evolution of love."

In spiritual science we say that the ancient Moon preceded the Earth. This ancient Moon, as a planetary stage of evolution, also had a mission. It did not yet have the task of developing love; it was the planet or the cosmos of wisdom. Before it reached our earthly condition, our planet passed through the stage of wisdom. A simple, and one might say logical, observation will illustrate this. Just look about you at all the creatures of nature. If you observe them not merely with your understanding but with the forces of your heart and soul, you will find wisdom everywhere stamped upon nature. The wisdom we are speaking of is a kind of spiritual substance lying at the foundation of all things. Observe anything you wish in nature, and you will find it there. Take, for example, a piece of the thighbone and you will see that it is not composed of a solid mass, but is a fine interweaving of supports arranged into a marvelous structure. And if we look for the law on which this bone is constructed, we find it is the development of the greatest strength with the least expenditure of material in order to be able to support the upper human body. Our engineering art is not yet advanced enough to build such a highly artistic structure as the one fashioned by the all-overruling wisdom. Humankind will not possess such wisdom until later in its evolution. Divine wisdom pervades the whole of nature; human wisdom will only gradually reach this height. In the course of time human wisdom will inwardly acquire what divine wisdom has secreted within the Earth. Just as wisdom was prepared on the Moon so that it might be found everywhere on the Earth, so is love now being prepared here in this Earth evolution. If you were able to look back upon the ancient Moon with clairvoyant vision, you would see that wisdom was not found everywhere at that time; you would find many things still lacking in wisdom. Only gradually throughout the Moon evolution was wisdom stamped upon the outer world. When the Moon had fully completed its evolution, everything was pervaded by a wisdom that was to be found everywhere. Inner wisdom first appeared on the Earth with the human being, with the I. This inner human wisdom had to be developed by degrees.

Just as wisdom was evolved upon the Moon, in order that it might now be found in all things, so in like manner is love evolving. Love came into existence first in its lowest, its most sensuous, form during the Lemurian period. During the course of life on the Earth, it will become ever more and more spiritualized, until at last, when the Earth has reached the end of its evolution, the whole of existence will have become pervaded with love, as today it is pervaded with wisdom. And this will be accomplished through the activity of human beings, if they but fulfil their task.

The Earth will then pass over to a future planetary condition called Jupiter. The beings who will wander about on Jupiter, just as human beings move about on Earth, will find love exhaling from all creatures, the love they themselves, as human beings, will have placed there during their life on Earth. They will find love in everything, just as we today find wisdom everywhere. Then human beings will develop love out of their own inner selves, in the same way they are now little by little evolving wisdom. The great cosmic love that is beginning its existence here on the Earth will then permeate all things. The materialistic mind does not believe in a cosmic wisdom, only in a human wisdom. If people would consider the course of evolution with unprejudiced minds, they would be able to see that all cosmic wisdom was as far advanced in the beginning of the Earth's evolution as human wisdom will be at the end of it. In times when names were more accurately chosen than they are today, the subjective wisdom active in the human being was called "intelligence," as distinct from objective cosmic wisdom. We do not notice that what we discover in the course of earthly life had already been won during life upon the Moon and implanted in the Earth by divine spiritual beings. Let us take an example.

How the great progress humankind has made through the discovery of paper is drummed into the heads of schoolchildren! But wasps had already produced paper many thousands of years ago, for they build their nests with exactly the same substance humans now use to produce paper, and the wasps produce it in exactly the same way—only by a life process. The wasp spirit, the group soul of the wasps, which is a part of divine spiritual substance, was the discoverer of paper long before humans made the discovery.

In fact, human beings always follow along, groping their way behind the cosmic wisdom. As a principle, all that human beings will discover in the course of the Earth's evolution is already present in nature. But what human beings will really give to the Earth is love, a love that will evolve from the most sensuous to the most spiritualized form. This is the mission of Earth evolution. Earth is the cosmos of love.

Let us ask, What then is essential for love? What is essential so that one person may love another? It is this—that he or she be in possession of full self-awareness, that he or she be wholly independent. No one can love another in the full sense of the word if this love is not a free gift of one person to another. My hand does not love my organism. Only one who is independent, who is not bound to the other person, can love another person. To this end the human being had to become an I-being. The I had to be implanted in the threefold human body so that the Earth might, through humankind, fulfil its mission of love. Therefore, you will understand esoteric Christianity when it says that, just as other forces, of which wisdom is the last, streamed down from divine beings during the Moon period, so now love streams into the Earth, and the bearer of love can only be the independent I that develops by degrees in the course of the evolution of the Earth.

Human beings had to be very slowly prepared for all this, likewise for their present kind of consciousness. Let us suppose, for instance, that human beings had been immersed in the physical body in the ancient Lemurian period—they would have seen the full outer reality at that time, but at such a swift tempo that they would not have been able to implant love in the world. They had to be guided little by little to their earthly mission. The first instruction in love was given them during the time of a dawning consciousness, before they possessed full self-awareness, before they were evolved far enough to observe the objects about them with clear, waking day-consciousness. Thus we see that during the ages when human beings still possessed an ancient, dreamy clairvoyant consciousness, when the soul was outside the physical body for long periods, love was being implanted within them in their dull, not yet self-aware condition. Let us clearly picture the soul of these human creatures of ancient times, which had not yet reached the height of full self-awareness.

Those human beings fell asleep at night, but there was no abrupt transition from waking to sleeping. Images emerged, vivid dream pictures, which, however, possessed a living relationship to the spirit world; this means that the human creatures familiarized themselves with the spirit world during sleep. The Divine Spirit dropped into them, into their dull state of consciousness, the first seed of all love activity. The power that manifests itself as love in the course of evolution on the Earth streamed at first into humankind during the night. The God who brought the true earthly mission to the Earth revealed itself first in the night to the dim, ancient clairvoyant consciousness before it could reveal itself to clear, waking day-consciousness.

Then, slowly and gradually, the time spent in a dim clairvoyant state of consciousness became shorter and shorter, and the time spent in day-consciousness became ever longer; the boundaries of the aura around physical objects gradually lessened and disappeared, and the objects took on clearer and clearer outlines. Formerly the Sun and the Moon were seen surrounded by mighty halos, as though lying in a mass of fog. Only slowly did the whole aspect become clear and objects assume distinct outlines. Human beings arrived at this condition by degrees. They then saw externally, by the visible light of the Sun shining upon the Earth, the whole of earth life, minerals, plants, and animals. All this they experienced as the revelations of the Divine in the outer world.

From the standpoint of esoteric Christianity, what is it that is visible during waking day-consciousness? In the broadest sense of the word, we may ask, What does the Earth consist of? It is a manifestation of divine powers, an outer material manifestation of inner spirituality. If you turn your gaze upward toward the Sun or toward what is to be found upon the Earth, you will see everywhere a manifestation of Divine Spirituality. This Divine Spirituality, in the present form, lies at the foundation of all that appears to clear, waking day-consciousness; in other words, it is the invisible world behind this entire visible day world. This is called in esoteric Christianity the "Logos" or the "Word." For just as speech can finally come forth from the human being, can be uttered from its own inner being, so too has everything—animal kingdom, plant kingdom, mineral kingdom—first come into existence from the Logos. Everything is an incarnation of the Logos, and just as your soul rules invisibly within your inner being and creates an external body, so too everything in the world of a soul nature creates for itself the external body fitted to it and manifests itself through some sort of physical organism. Where, then, is the physical body of the Logos, of which the Gospel of St. John speaks? It is this we wish to bring more and more into our consciousness today. In its purest form, this external physical body of the Logos appears especially in the outer sunlight. But the sunlight is not merely material light. To spiritual perception, it is just as much the vesture of the Logos as your outer physical body is the vesture of your soul.

If you confronted a human being the way the greater part of humanity today confronts the Sun, you could never learn to know that person. Your relation to each human individual possessing a feeling, thinking, and willing soul would be such that instead of presupposing that person had an inner psycho-spiritual part, you would simply touch a physical body and imagine that it might even be made of papier-mâché. If, however, you wish to penetrate to the spiritual in the sunlight, you should consider it just as you consider the bodily part of a human being in order to learn to know the person's inner nature. The sunlight has the same relationship to the Logos as your body has to your soul. Something spiritual streams down upon the Earth in the sunlight. If we are able to conceive not only the Sun body, but also the Sun spirit, we find that the spiritual part is the love that streams down upon the Earth. The physical sunlight alone does not awaken plants into life; they would wither and die if the physical sunlight did not act upon them, but together with the physical sunlight, the warm love of the Godhead streams to Earth. Human beings exist so that they may take into themselves the warm love of the Divine, develop it, and return it to the Divine. But they can only do this by becoming self-aware I-beings. Only then will they be able to render back this love.

When human beings began, at first for a very short time, to live in waking consciousness, they could perceive nothing of the light, the light that at the same time enkindled love. The light shone into the darkness, but the darkness was unable yet to comprehend it. If this light, which is at the same time the love of the Logos, had manifested itself only during the short day hours, humankind would not have been able to grasp it. But love streamed into human beings in the dull clairvoyant dream consciousness of those ancient times. Now, let us glance behind existence at a great cosmic mystery.

Let us express it this way: The cosmic guidance of our Earth was of such a character that for a time, in an unconscious way, love streamed into humankind in its dim, clairvoyant state of consciousness and inwardly prepared it to receive this love in full, clear, waking day-consciousness. We have seen that our Earth gradually became the cosmos that was to accomplish this mission of love. The Earth is shone upon by the present Sun. Just as human beings dwell upon the Earth and, little by little, receive love into themselves, so too do other much higher beings dwell upon the Sun and enkindle love, because the Sun has reached a higher stage of existence. The human being is an Earth dweller and to be an Earth dweller means to be a creature that appropriates love unto itself during the Earth period. A Sun dweller in our time means a being that can enkindle love, a being that can permit love to flow into the Earth. The Earth dwellers would not have developed love, would not have been able to receive it, had not the Sun dwellers sent down ripened wisdom to them with the rays of light. Because the light of the Sun streams down upon the Earth, love is developed there. That is a very real truth. Beings who are so exalted that they can pour forth love have made the Sun their scene of action.

When the ancient Moon had completed its evolution, there were seven great beings of this kind who had progressed far enough to pour forth love. Here we touch upon a deep mystery revealed by spiritual science. In the beginning of the Earth's evolution, there was on the one side the childlike humankind, which was to receive love and become ready for the reception of the I, and on the other side was the Sun, which separated from the Earth and rose to a more exalted existence. Seven principle Spirits of Light, who at the same time were the dispensing Spirits of Love, were able to evolve upon this Sun. However, only six of them made the Sun their dwelling place, and what streams down to us in the physical light of the Sun contains the spiritual force of love from these six Spirits of Light or, as they are called in the Bible, the six Elohim. One separated from the others and took a different path for the salvation of humankind. He choose not the Sun but the Moon for his abode. And this Spirit of Light, who voluntarily renounced life upon the Sun and chose the Moon instead, is none other than the one the Old Testament calls "Jahweh" or "Jehovah." This Spirit of Light who chose the Moon as a dwelling place is the one who from there pours ripened wisdom down upon the Earth, thus preparing the way for love. Now, let us consider for a moment a mystery behind the outer facts.

The night belongs to the Moon, and it belonged to the Moon to a much greater degree in that ancient time when human beings were not yet able to receive the force of love in the direct rays of the Sun. At that time they received the reflected force of ripened wisdom from the moonlight. This ripened wisdom streamed down upon them from the moonlight during the time of night-consciousness. Therefore, Jahweh is called the Ruler of the Night, who prepared humankind for the love that was later to manifest during full waking consciousness. Thus we can look back to that ancient past in human evolution when the spiritual event occurred that is merely symbolized by the heavenly bodies, the Sun on one side, the Moon on the other. (See drawing.) During the night, at certain times, the Moon sends down to us the reflected force of the Sun, but it is the same light that also shines upon us directly from the Sun. Thus in ancient times Jahweh, or Jehovah, reflected the force of matured wisdom, the force of the six Elohim, and sent it down into human beings while they slept, preparing them to become capable later, by degrees, of receiving the power of love during waking day-consciousness.

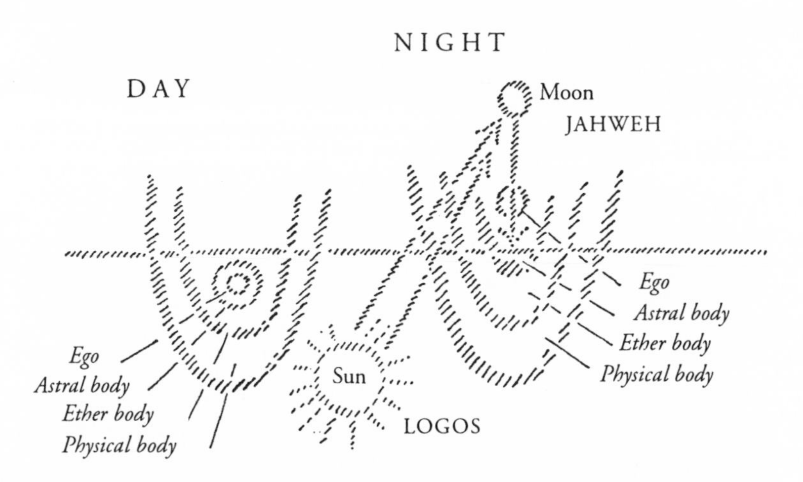

The above drawing attempts to show in a symbolic way the waking-day human being when the physical and etheric bodies are dependent upon the Divine and the I and the astral body are within the physical and ether bodies upon the physical plane. Here the whole human organism is shone upon by the Sun from without. We now know that for the human beings of primeval ages, night was much longer and much more filled with activity than it is at present. The astral body and the I were then outside the physical and ether bodies; the I existed wholly within the astral world, and the astral body sank into the physical body from without, but had its entire inner being still embedded in the divine spiritual world. Therefore, the Sun could not shine directly upon the human astral body and enkindle the force of love in it. Hence, the Moon, which reflects the sunlight, was active through Jahweh, or Jehovah. The Moon is the symbol of Jahweh, or Jehovah, and the Sun is none other than the symbol for the Logos, which is the sum of the other six Elohim. This drawing, which you should study and meditate on, tries to indicate this in a symbolic way, and if you reflect upon it, you will discern what deep, mystery truths are presented in it. Namely, during long periods of time the force of love was being implanted by Jehovah in human beings in sleep consciousness, in a manner they were unconscious of. In this way they were being made capable of experiencing the Logos, of feeling the force of its love. One can ask, How was this possible, how could that take place? We come now to the other side of the mystery.

We have said that human beings were destined for self-aware love upon the Earth. They must, therefore, have a leader, a teacher, during their clear day-consciousness, a leader who stands before them and can be perceived by them. Now it was only during the night, in dim consciousness, that love could be implanted within human beings. But little by little something happened; something happened in full actuality that made it possible for them to see outwardly, physically, the Being of Love itself. But how could that occur? It could take place only because the Being of Divine Love, the Being of the Logos, became a man of flesh, whom humans, through their physical senses, could perceive upon the Earth. It was because humankind had developed to a condition of perceiving by means of outer senses that God, the Logos, had to become a sense being. He had to appear in a physical body. This was fulfilled in Christ Jesus, and the historical appearance of Christ Jesus means that the forces of the six Elohim, or of the Logos, were incarnated in Jesus of Nazareth at the beginning of our Christian era and were actually present in him in the visible world. That is the important thing. The inner force of the Sun, the force of the Logos-Love, assumed a physical human form in the body of Jesus of Nazareth. For God had to appear to the earthly human sense consciousness in a bodily form like an external object, like an outer being.

You will ask, what was the Being who appeared at the beginning of our era as Christ Jesus? It was the incarnation of the Logos, of the six other Elohim, whose advent had been prepared by Jahweh-God who preceded them. This figure of Jesus of Nazareth, in whom the Christ or the Logos was incarnated, brought into human life, into human history itself, what previously streamed down upon Earth from the Sun, what was present only in the sunlight. "The Logos became flesh." It is upon this fact that the Gospel of St. John places the greatest importance, and the writer of this Gospel had to lay great emphasis upon it because it is a fact that after the appearance of a few initiated Christian pupils who understood what had occurred, others followed who could not fully understand it. They understood full well that at the foundation of all material things, behind all that appears to us in substantial form, is a psycho-spiritual world. But what they could not comprehend was that the Logos itself, by incarnating in an individual human being, became physically visible for the physical sense-world. This they could not comprehend. Therefore, the teaching called "Gnosis," which appeared in the early Christian centuries, differs from true esoteric Christianity on this point. The writer of the Gospel of St. John pointed to this fact in powerful words, when he said: "No, you should not look upon the Christ only as a supersensible, ever invisible being, the foundation of all material life; rather you should consider this the important thing: The Word became flesh and dwelt among us." This is the fine distinction between esoteric Christianity and the primal Gnosis. Gnosis, as well as esoteric Christianity, recognizes the Christ, but the former sees him as only a spiritual being and sees Jesus of Nazareth as at most a human herald, more or less bound to this spiritual being. Gnosis holds firmly to an ever invisible Christ. Esoteric Christianity, on the contrary, has always held the idea of the Gospel of St. John, which rests upon the firm foundation of the words, "And the Logos became flesh and dwelt among us!" He who was there in the visible world is an actual incarnation of the six Sun Elohim, of the Logos! With the incarnation of the Logos, the earthly mission—or in other words, what the Earth was to become through the event of Palestine—first really began. Everything previous was only preparation.

What then did the Christ, who dwelt within the body of Jesus of Nazareth, especially have to represent himself to be? It may be said that he had to represent himself as the great bringer and quickener of the self-aware, independent human being. Let us express this living teaching of Christ in a few short, paradigmatic sentences. The earth exists so that full self-awareness, the "I AM," may be given to humankind. Everything previous was a preparation for this self-awareness, for this "I AM"; and the Christ was the being who gave the impulse that made it possible for every human being—each as an individual—to experience the "I AM." Only with his advent was the powerful impulse given that carries Earth humankind forward with a mighty bound. We can follow this by comparing Christianity with the Old Testament teaching. In the latter, human beings did not yet fully feel the "I AM" in themselves. They still possessed a remnant of a dreamy state of consciousness, held over from those ancient times when they did not feel themselves as personalities, but as a part of a Divine Being, just as the animal today is still a member of a group soul. Humankind had its beginning in the group soul and then advanced to a state of independent, personal existence in which every individual experiences the "I AM"; and the Christ is the force that has brought it to this consciousness of the "I AM." Let us consider this for a moment in its full inner significance.

Followers of the Old Testament did not feel themselves as much enclosed within their own individual personalities as did followers of the New Testament. They did not yet say as a personality, "I am an I." They felt themselves within the whole ancient Jewish people and experienced the group I of their folk. Let us enter in a living way into the consciousness of the followers of the Old Testament. Christians feel the "I AM" and gradually will learn to feel it more and more, but followers of the Old Testament did not feel the "I AM" in this way. They felt themselves to be members of the entire folk and looked up to its group soul. And if they wished to express this in words, they would have said, "My consciousness reaches up to the Father of the whole people, to Abraham; we—I and Father Abraham—are one. A common I encompasses us all, and I only feel myself safe within the spiritual substantiality of the world when I feel myself resting within the whole folk-substance." Thus followers of the Old Testament looked up to Father Abraham and said, "I and Father Abraham are one! In my veins flows the same blood that flows in the veins of Abraham." They felt Father Abraham to be the root from which every individual Abrahamite had sprung as a stem.

Then Christ Jesus came and said to his nearest, most intimate initiates: Hitherto, humankind has judged only according to the flesh, according to blood relationship. Through this blood relationship, human beings have been conscious of reposing within a higher invisible union. But you should believe in a still higher spiritual relationship, in one that reaches beyond the blood tie. You should believe in a spiritual Father-substance in which the I is rooted. It is more spiritual than the substance that, as a group soul, binds the Jewish people together. You should believe in what reposes within me and within every human being, in what is not only one with Abraham, but one with the very divine foundation of the world. Therefore Christ Jesus, according to the Gospel of St. John, emphasizes the words, "Before Father Abraham was, was the I AM!" Not only does my primal I mount to the Father Principle that reaches back to Abraham, but it is also one with all that pulses through the entire cosmos, and to this my spiritual nature soars aloft. I and the Father are one! These are important words that one should experience; then one will feel the forward bound made by humankind, a bound that advanced human evolution further due to the impulse given by the advent of the Christ. The Christ was the mighty quickener of the "I AM."

Now, let us try to hear a little of what his most intimate initiates said, how they expressed what had been revealed to them. They said, Heretofore, no individual physical human being has ever existed to whom the name "I AM" could be applied; he was the first to bring to the world the "I AM" in its full significance. Therefore, they named Christ Jesus the "I AM." That was the name in which the closest initiates felt themselves united, the name they understood: the name "I AM." We must in this way delve deeply into the most significant chapters of the Gospel of St. John. If we take the chapter where we find the words, "I am the Light of the world," we must interpret them literally, quite literally. Now, what was this "I AM" that for the first time appeared incarnated? It was the force of the Logos that streamed to Earth in the sunlight. Beginning with the twelfth verse, we find all through the eighth chapter, usually entitled "Jesus, the Light of the World," a transcription of this profound truth about the meaning of the "I AM." When you read this chapter, emphasize the words "I" or "I AM" wherever they appear, and realize that "I AM" was the name through which the initiates felt themselves united. Then you will understand it and it will seem to you that this chapter must be read in somewhat the following manner:

> Then Jesus spoke to his disciples and said, Whatever can say to itself "I AM" is the Force of the Light of the World; and whoever follows me will see in clear, waking consciousness what those who wander in darkness do not see.
>
> But the Pharisees—those who clung to the old belief that the Light of Love can be implanted within the human being only at night—answered: You call on your "I AM," but we call on Father Abraham. In this way we feel the power that justifies us in acting as self-aware beings. We feel strong when we immerse ourselves in the substance of a common I-being that reaches to Father Abraham.
>
> Jesus said: If one speaks of I-being as I speak, then is that testimony true; for I know that this I comes from the Father, from the primeval foundation of the world, and I know where it tends. (John 8:12–14)

Now, let us consider those important words of chapter 8, verse 15, which should be translated as follows:

> You judge all things according to the flesh, but I judge not the perishable that is in the flesh.
>
> And if I judge, then is my judgment true. For the I does not exist for itself alone, but is united with the Father from whom it has descended. (John 8:15–16)

This is the meaning of that passage. Thus everywhere you find reference to a common Father. Now we are able to bring the idea of the Father even more clearly before our souls. Then we see the words, "Before Father Abraham was, was the I AM," and we know they contain the living essence of the Christian doctrine....

5.

LOVE: THE MISSION OF THE EARTH II

AUGUST 12, 1908, STUTTGART

from *Universe, Earth, and Man*

IN order to understand our subject more thoroughly, let's direct our gaze first toward the great universe and then toward the more limited sphere of our own immediate, earthly existence. In this way we shall be able to accurately picture what spiritual, or esoteric, science understands as the three concepts of *universe*, *Earth*, and the *human being*.

You will have gathered from what has been said that, according to spiritual science, the we cannot think that the world consists only of matter. We have encountered various world *entities* (it is better not to speak of our Earth's various embodiments, "Old Saturn," "Old Sun," and "Old Moon," as world "bodies"); and we have heard how they are certainly not simply material substance. This applies also to what we describe as the contrast between the Earth as a planet and the Sun as a fixed star. Each world entity has been, as we have seen, the dwelling of a host of spiritual beings, created to meet their particular needs.

The Sun separated from the Earth because it had to become the home of certain exalted beings who could use only the finer substances for their evolution, whereas human beings, on the other hand, had to retain the other substances on the Earth. If we were to investigate the whole, wide universe we would find nothing solely material; everything is connected with spirit. We heard, too, how various earthly beings are related to spiritual beings. The Earth's stones and minerals have their I-being in the surrounding universe. Plants have their I-being in the center of the Earth, whereas their astral being (which brings about the formation of blossoms) hovers outside them. The fact that everything is pervaded by spirit widens and enriches our notions, or our image, of a cosmic body. We look up at a body in the heavens and become aware that it is simply the expression of spiritual beings materially connected with it.

Now, the development of certain dormant faculties within human beings enables them to gain knowledge of these heavenly bodies spread out in space; today we shall consider humankind's connection with these bodies.

On our Earth we are surrounded by minerals, plants, animals, and other human companions. We also know that earthly affairs are regulated by higher beings, who, in Christian terminology, are called *Angels*, *Archangels*, and *Archai*. We also know that there are other beings concerned with the Earth, although they send their forces from the Sun or the Moon. Today we can add to this. The question arises: To what extent may the essential being of one planet in our solar system be compared with another?

To simplify matters, let us consider the beings we can see around us in our present cycle of human evolution and ask, How are the beings that surround us here as minerals, plants, animals, and humans related to other beings in the universe?

We are, of course, approaching this question in a spiritual scientific way, from knowledge acquired through the development of clairvoyant consciousness, to which I shall return later. First, let us ask, Does clairvoyant consciousness find on other planets human beings similar to those evolving on our Earth? Clairvoyant consciousness answers that we do not find human beings on other planets in exactly the same form as on Earth, but we do find strong confirmation that each planet, each heavenly body, has its own particular task and mission. Nothing is repeated in the universe; every heavenly body has a different mission.

Our Earth has arisen from three preceding embodiments. The human stage of existence we ourselves are now passing through has been passed through by other beings—for example, by the Angels on Old Moon, by the Archangels (Spirits of Fire) on Old Sun, and by the Archai (Spirits of Personality) on Old Saturn. It is easy to make the mistake of thinking that these beings were human beings like ourselves in the preceding planetary embodiments. But it must be borne in mind that there was no solid rock or minerals on Old Moon and that therefore the beings who went through their human stage there did so under entirely different conditions. The Archangels (Spirits of Fire), for example, passed through their human stage in utterly different conditions, since Old Sun consisted only of gas and air. Only beings who, unlike us, had no need of solid bodies, muscles, and so on, could pass through their human stage there. In earthly evolution, too, nothing is repeated, and every stage has its particular mission in the great household of cosmic existence.

Let us now consider first the evolution of our Earth. With spiritual vision, we see it as a body inhabited by human beings, where they are evolving. This evolving became possible only because the Sun and the Moon separated from the Earth, resulting in humankind's forces being held in balance between Sun and Moon. When the Earth was still Sun, so to speak, it passed through a phase of evolution in union with the Sun. The Sun itself was thus still at the stage of planetary existence and was inhabited by the Spirits of Fire. But progressive development made it possible for the part of the Sun that was incorporated in the Earth to rise to a higher state of existence at the expense of the remainder, which separated off as the Earth's Moon. In the great universe evolution proceeds in this way: things that for a time have progressed side by side then separate, one rising into higher spheres, the other descending into a lower state. In order for certain higher beings to develop to a sufficiently lofty stage, the Sun itself had to become a suitable arena for them, so it advanced from a planetary existence to that of a fixed star. We must therefore consider our Sun to be a cosmic being that has evolved from a planet. Viewed in the light of esotericism, the Sun is a planet that has risen to a higher state of existence.

As was indicated in yesterday's lecture, after the Sun had separated from Earth-plus-Moon, humankind continued to live for a period within this more restricted Earth existence, without the spiritual forces of the Sun. Then, with the coming of Christ, the spiritual Sun force took root upon our Earth. As the consequence of Christ's embodiment with the Earth, human beings will become ever more mature by receiving the Christ Principle into themselves; and the material form taken on by a planet is dependent on the kind of beings it develops.

Just as the Sun became what it is by withdrawing the finest substances because its beings needed them, so too will the Earth. The substances of the Earth will by then have been transformed so as to be suited to the being that humans will have become in the distant future, together with the other Earth beings they bear along with them; for when human beings become truly strong they will draw the other beings after them.

What will happen then? If humans imbue themselves more fully with the Christ Principle, if they absorb more and more of the exalted Sun forces that descended with Christ to the Earth, they will themselves become more Christlike and will irradiate the whole Earth with the Christ Principle.

What is this Christ Principle? We need to be very clear about this, and for this we must know what the mission of our Earth is so that we can describe the latter by one specific word. What is the mission of our earthly existence? What, for example, was the mission of Old Moon, which preceded Earth?

If we look back at Old Moon clairvoyantly, we find at the beginning of its existence something very remarkable in the forerunners of the beings on our Earth. They had many qualities, but at the beginning of the Old Moon embodiment they lacked one in particular that we now find all around us in our Earth existence. The forces of Old Moon, the precursor of our Earth, worked together without wisdom; at the beginning of this period things were still such that no sign of harmonious cooperation born of wisdom could have been observed. But if we follow the evolution of Old Moon clairvoyantly we see how wisdom, drawn from the cosmos, was instilled in the beings dwelling there by other beings active in Old Moon's surroundings. Old Moon is therefore called the Planet of Wisdom.

When the Old Moon period ended, wisdom was in all things. The Old Moon embodiment then passed through an intermediate condition resembling a world sleep, known as *pralaya*, emerging again as Earth existence; and when the beings emerged from this condition they brought with them the wisdom that had been instilled in them on Old Moon. The consequence of this is that wisdom is implanted in all earthly beings. In all the beings around us that stem from the Old Moon embodiment and have yet a further mission, wisdom is evident. Look where you will; take, for example, the blossom of any plant. The more closely you look at it, the more wonderful it appears, for the arrangement of the several parts is the result of higher wisdom. Take the human thighbone. See how the highest wisdom has ordered the constituent parts to form a support capable of carrying the upper part of the body. No modern engineering skill in bridge construction can match the sublime wisdom manifest in that bone structure. In all the other human organs, and indeed in all that surrounds us, we see wisdom at the root of all things.

One could say in a stumbling kind of way that earthly humankind should at first absorb this wisdom into its inner self. Microcosmic wisdom can be learned only from the objects that surround humans here. Yet wisdom is inherent in all things, even in the parts of the human constitution where we do not function consciously.

In speaking of historical development we often extol human wisdom. How wonderful it seems when we learn at school that at a particular time humankind made this or that invention or discovery. Many of us have been taught, for example, that in recent times humans discovered the art of papermaking with their human intelligence—but wasps could do this long before humans. It is true, of course, that it is not the individual wasp but the group soul of the wasps that constructs the nest from the same material as our paper. These group souls possessed long ago what human beings will gain only gradually. The wisdom that is deeply ingrained in all beings on Earth had to be implanted gradually. We shall see how this came about during the Old Moon existence, how at that time wisdom battled against non-wisdom, and how Old Moon then bequeathed to the Earth rudimentary beings in whom wisdom had been implanted.

What is to be similarly implanted into the beings of our Earth? Just as wisdom was implanted during the Old Moon embodiment, love is to be implanted on our planet. Our planet is the Planet of Love. The initial development, the first infusing with love, began in its lowest form. This happened during the Lemurian epoch when the human I took shape; at that time the development of love in its lowest form began with the separation of the sexes. And all further development consists in continual refinement of this love principle to the point of spiritualization. Just as wisdom was instilled in all beings during the Old Moon embodiment, so one day, when our Earth has attained its goal, all earthly beings will be filled with love.

Let us now think for a moment of the planetary existence that will follow our Earth, that of Jupiter. When the beings who will inhabit Jupiter reappear, they will perceive with their own spiritual faculties the beings surrounding them. And just as we, with our intellect, admire the wisdom inherent in stones, plants, and animals, indeed in everything around us—just as we draw wisdom from them for our own benefit—so will the Jupiter beings direct their forces to the beings in their environment and have the love that was implanted in those beings during Earth evolution wafted back to them. Just as we analyze objects and are edified by their inherent wisdom, the Jupiter beings will be edified by the outpourings of love from the beings around them. This love, which is to develop on Earth, can develop only through earthly I-beings interrelated in the way described. Only through severance from the group soul could this development begin, with one being facing another being; only in this way could true love develop. No true love is possible where the I-beings are interconnected within the group soul. Beings must be distinct from each other and offer love as a free gift. Only through a separation like the one that has come about in the human kingdom, where I meets I as independent individuals, has love as a free offering become possible. This is why increasing individualization and the union of distinct individuals had to come about on the Earth.

Let us think about beings belonging to a group soul; their actions are directed by the group soul. Can it be said that the heart loves the stomach? No, the heart is united to the stomach by the inner being that holds them together. In the same way the animal species are united with each other within a group soul, and their activities are regulated by the wisdom of the group soul. Only when this group nature is surmounted and an individual I faces another individual I, can the sympathy present as love be offered as a free gift from one being to another.

Human beings had to be prepared gradually for this mission, and we see that, before becoming fully individualized, they went through a kind of preliminary training for this love. We see how, before they possessed an I completely, they were gathered into blood-related groups by the beings that guided them; members of these groups loved one another because of the blood tie. This was the great era of preparation for humanity. It has already been pointed out that at this stage love was not yet a gift to be made freely but was directed by a remnant of cosmic wisdom. We have heard how luciferic beings were active here, opposing with a strong liberating force everything that gathered humanity together in tribes and peoples through the power of the blood. All the forces striving to make humans independent operated through the luciferic spirits.

Thus human beings continued to mature so that in the fullness of time they might receive love in its highest potency, in the Christ Principle, whose essence is expressed in the words, "He who loves father or mother more than me is not worthy of me; and he who loves son or daughter more than me is not worthy of me; and he who does not take up his cross and follow me is not worthy of me" [Matt. 10:37–38]. These words are not to be understood in any trite way. Their meaning is that through the Christ Principle the old blood relationship was to assume new forms of belonging together that would pass from soul to soul, from individual to individual, irrespective of a material basis. The Christ Principle has given the impulse for one person to love another; thus, through being Christianized, human love will become increasingly spiritual. Love will become more of the nature of soul and then spirit, and through this human beings will draw along with them the lower beings of the Earth and will transform the whole Earth. In a remote future they will transform the entire substance of the Earth, making the Earth's body mature again for reuniting with the Sun. Christ, the spiritual Sun, has given the impulse toward the reuniting of the Sun and the Earth in one body at some future time.

We have seen, in surveying the course of world evolution, how the Sun first separated physically from the Earth and how the mighty impulse of the Christ Principle was then sent down to Earth to provide the impetus for a reuniting of Earth and Sun so that they might ascend to higher stages of existence. We have also realized that our Earth can harbor only those human beings who have this as their mission. Therefore, when we survey the human kingdom desiring to learn about earthly humankind, we can find it only on the Earth, for it was here that appropriate conditions were created for such human beings as now exist here.

But what of the other kingdoms? Let us consider first that of the plants. Clairvoyant vision, observing our world and examining the other planets belonging to our solar system, finds on all of them a plant kingdom like ours; so in our plant kingdom we have something that exists throughout our solar system.

Thus we find that our solar system is populated by plant beings, and if we looked at the matter with esoteric knowledge, we would see that each planet is populated with its own kind of human beings. It is easy to perceive a close relationship between plants and the Sun, and also how plant existence is intimately connected with that of the Sun. But if this is so, the same must hold true for all the plants in our solar system. Looking back to the time when the Earth was still the Sun planet (the old Sun embodiment), we know that at that time human beings consisted of a physical body and an etheric body—they were at the plant stage of existence, at the level of the plant kingdom surrounding us today, which is composed of beings consisting of a physical body and an etheric body. In our encounters with these beings we feel we can say that they have remained true to the Sun; even today they manifest quite clearly their connection with the Sun.

Let us consider such a plant being according to Rosicrucian wisdom. We see how the plant is fixed in the ground by its root, the organ that points it toward the center of the Earth—to its I—while its reproductive organs are turned toward the Sun, absorbing its pure rays.

Now let us think of the human being. It is not difficult to picture the human being as a reversed plant. If we think of a plant exactly reversed in position, we have the human being; its reproductive organs are directed toward the Earth's center, and its roots toward cosmic space. The animal stands halfway between these positions. Hence it can be said in a spiritual sense that when the soul element of the universe passed through the various kingdoms it went through plant, animal, and human existence. Plato expressed this in a wonderful way: "The world soul is crucified on the cross of the world body."[1]

During its plant stage of evolution, the human being was turned toward the center of the Earth. The corresponding direction for the animal is that of its spine—horizontal. The human being's position is that of the plant in reverse. This is the origin of the cross. The world soul is crucified; this is the meaning of the cross.

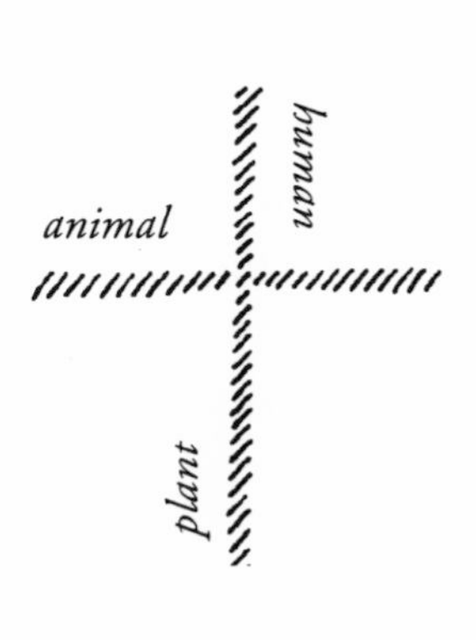

The plant of today is a being that strives toward the Sun, that has remained to a certain extent united with the Sun. Hence its orientation is the reverse of the human being's. Animal forms in the various planetary existences are sometimes similar and sometimes different: in this respect, too, the animal stands halfway between the human being and the plant.

Turning now to the mineral kingdom, we find that there is something in the forms of crystals that takes us into cosmic space, beyond our solar system's borders. When we consider

1. Plato, *Timaeus*, chapter 8.

translucent mineral formations in particular, we gain an inkling of what goes on in the universe far beyond the boundaries of our solar system. The mineral, something extremely abstract, seemingly with no definite existence, and yet the very foundation of our life, has a cosmic existence. The more exalted the beings, the more they are suited to our Earth's solar system.

We will now consider the same question in relation to the human being. If human beings were adapted only to the forces prevailing on Earth, they would be condemned to exist there and there alone; they could never make themselves into citizens of the universe; they could never speak of anything that transcended the earthly. Although they are adapted in their external form to the conditions pertaining on Earth, they have, through their higher powers, a part in the higher beings linked with the Earth. What restricts human beings to the Earth relates only to their body; the spiritual powers with which they are endowed lead them far beyond the Earth. Here again we must distinguish between widely differing forces. Let us deal first with those that can be easily distinguished.

First, there is the power that in spiritual vision we saw arise in pre-Atlantean times. Human consciousness, to begin with, was a picture consciousness, and it was not until later on in earthly evolution that humans became able to grasp external objects with objective consciousness. This consciousness—which today presents the world of the senses to us so that we can see colors, hear sounds, smell, and taste—became differentiated from the general awareness of warmth perceived by the organ that was a kind of lantern, the pineal gland. Objective consciousness is entirely of the Earth. Such sensory perception may be found only on Earth. Strange as it may seem, all our sense perceptions, such as those of color, sound, and so forth, have only earthly existence, and were we to encounter the beings of other planets we would find ourselves at a loss to make ourselves intelligible to them. For instance, if we were to say something to those beings about the color red they would not know what was meant; on their planet they have a different way of perceiving objects and beings. What we call sensory perception is of service only on our particular planet.

We have already heard that before sense perception became a specific faculty it was inwardly connected with fertilization. Just as our sense perception is of the Earth, so too the process of human fertilization, as it exists today, belongs exclusively to the Earth and is adapted only to this planetary embodiment. It exists in order to provide a basis for the mission of the Earth, namely love, for it is on the Earth that love is to develop. Here we have an external human faculty that pertains to the Earth alone.

We come now to another power or faculty. Suppose you are looking at some object. As long as your eyes are directed to the object you know that you are connected with it in some way; it has an effect on you. Now turn away and keep its picture in your memory; the object has gone but its picture stays with you. If humans could not retain such pictures they would be an entirely different being, for as soon as they looked away from an object the mental picture of it would also disappear. Consequently they would not be able to combine the characteristics of the observed object.

The capacity of consciousness that enables humans today to retain the picture of an object that is elsewhere was already theirs on Old Moon; it is the same faculty that then enabled them to see what was around them in pictures. They could not at that time perceive external objects as they do today, but if they approached some object an astral vision arose before them like a vivid dream picture, which nevertheless stood in a definite relationship to the object.

Human beings then possessed a pictorial and not an objective consciousness. Nowadays we are in touch with the object; our picture of it envelops the object. A last remnant of picture consciousness remains in our power to form memory pictures.

These are, moreover, of greater value than the mere observation of external objects. If you observe a number of similar objects, you group them under a general concept. For example, here are many pieces of chalk, which you group under the general concept "chalk." In this way we evolve general concepts for which no external objects exist. We can work inwardly with our mental pictures, and if with this inner activity, this capacity for ideation, we were to come into contact with beings outside our own planetary existence, we would be able to make ourselves more easily understood. The picture consciousness, which was really a dim clairvoyance, that human beings had before they could perceive external objects, as well as the imaginative consciousness that they will develop later on, are both more comprehensive [than mere sensory perception].

When, through spiritual development, one has acquired picture consciousness and is able to perceive not only external objects but also a human aura, for example—when one sees in pictures the world of soul and spirit, and what exists in the world rises in pictorial symbols—then with this [Imaginative] consciousness one has acquired the ability to establish contact with other beings inhabiting the planetary universe.

There is a still higher degree of consciousness. Human beings had it in a dim form during the Old Sun period and still have it in a dim form in dreamless sleep. Humans are not entirely without consciousness when asleep. Neither is a plant devoid of consciousness—its day consciousness is the same as that of humans in sleep. Sleep is simply a lower stage of consciousness; things escape our attention and we cannot observe them.

By developing certain faculties human beings can acquire the power to perceive what is around them during the dreamless sleep state. This is a higher state of consciousness than that of picture consciousness; it is the consciousness possessed by plants, but in a dormant state. If individuals rise to this state of consciousness and pervade it with their I in full daylight consciousness, they have attained in esoteric development the stage of Inspiration, of inspired consciousness. This inspired consciousness does not work only in the form of pictures. When something flows from the object to the observer, it is a tone consciousness and cannot be compared to picture consciousness. Those who experience it enter a spiritual world of tones; this is the consciousness described by Pythagoras as the harmony of the spheres. The whole universe then resounds. When human beings fall asleep and the astral body and the I withdraw from the physical and etheric bodies, the harmonies and themes of cosmic music pervade the astral body. The astral body is then embedded in its true spiritual form of existence and acquires from the music of the spheres the ability to restore its run-down forces. Humans plunge at night into the music of the spheres, and because of the tones that resound through them, they awake in the morning newly refreshed and strengthened. And when they can make this conscious they have attained Inspiration and are capable of perceiving everything contained within their solar system.

Through the normal process of thought we perceive only the things of the Earth, but one is able through Imagination to come into contact with the beings of the various planets; and one who has attained Inspiration comes into a relationship with the solar system. This has always been known in certain circles. Goethe, who was an unconscious initiate, knew it; hence in the prologue to *Faust,* in a scene set in the spiritual world, heaven, he has the Angels proclaim:

> The Sun intones his ancient song,
> 'Mid rival chant of brother spheres.

This reveals that Goethe knew that the secrets of a solar system are expressed in tones and that whoever can achieve Inspiration becomes acquainted with these secrets. That he did not write these lines by chance is shown in part 2 where Faust is taken up into the spiritual world and the theme is repeated:

> Sounding loud to spirit ears.
> Lo! the newborn day appears.

"Spirit ears" are those of a clairvoyant able to perceive the sphere harmonies of a solar system. And if you could observe the Sun forces as they stream down onto the bodies of plants as they grow out of the Earth—these plants with their roots and leaves ending above with blossoms enveloped by astrality, into which the spiritual Sun forces pour—if you could perceive with a spiritual eye these forces that enter mysteriously through the blossom, you would "hear" them as the spiritual music of the spheres, audible, it is true, only to "spirit ears." Spiritual tones penetrate mysteriously into the flowers of plants. This is the secret of plant growth; each individual blossom is an expression of tones that give it its form and the fruit its character. The Sun's tones are caught up by the plant and reign within it as spirit.

You know, perhaps, how form can be created in the material world through sound. Think only of Chladni's sound figures, how powder scattered over a plate takes on certain patterns or figures when subjected to sound.[2] These figures are the expression of the sound that caused them. Just as physical sound is caught in this powder, the spiritual sound of the Sun is captured and drawn in by flower and fruit. It is hidden mysteriously within the seed, and when the new plant springs from the seed it is this trapped and absorbed sound that conjures forth the form of the plant.

Clairvoyant consciousness surveys our surrounding world of plants, and in the flowers that carpet our Earth's surface it sees everywhere the reflex of the Sun tones. What Goethe says is true, "The Sun intones his ancient song"; but it is also true that these Sun tones stream down, are absorbed by the plants, and reappear when the new plant springs from the seed. For the Sun tones resound in the forms of the plants, reechoing into space the music of the spheres.

There is a still higher state of consciousness, which we call Intuition, in the true sense of the word; by means of this human beings can penetrate into the very nature of things. This is beyond Inspiration; with Intuition people enter other beings directly and identify their very self with them. This leads them still further. Where can this inspirational [Intuitive] consciousness lead? It can lead people to feel they are one with their planet Earth, for the I-beings of the plants are at the center of the Earth. If people hear the sound of the Sun they become one

2. Ernst Chladni (1756–1827), German physicist known for studies of acoustics; he studied the vibration of strings and rods, and, through the use of sand, the vibration of plates.

with the planetary being embodied in the center of the Earth; they become one with their planet. But they can become one with every single being that exists. They then have experiences that reach beyond our solar system; their view widens from system consciousness to cosmic consciousness. Intuition transcends particular solar systems.

Thus we see that in the mineral kingdom there is something that, in its unified form, furnishes a basis extending far beyond our ordinary existence. We see that the present human form is a physical-earthly form, but that human beings will raise themselves once more from ordinary earthly consciousness to planetary consciousness through Imagination, to system consciousness through Inspiration, and to cosmic consciousness through Intuition.

This is humanity's path, for this path is bound up with the whole evolution of our universe.

6.

LOVE: THE MISSION OF THE EARTH III

MAY 14, 1912, BERLIN

from *Earthly and Cosmic Human Being*

THE question of the meaning and purpose of existence frequently arises in life and in the sphere of philosophy. Study of spiritual science will certainly produce a kind of humility in regard to this question, for although we know that investigation of the spiritual worlds leads thought and perception beyond the material sense world, we also realize that it is not possible to speak immediately about the primal origins or the ultimate and highest meaning of life. Here, the retort of superficial thinking will certainly be, What, then, do we know, if knowledge of the meaning and purpose of life is beyond our reach?

An analogy that is entirely in line with the attitude of spiritual science and indicates what is permissible or not permissible regarding this question, can be put in the following way: Suppose you want to journey somewhere. In your hometown you can get information only about how to reach a much nearer place, but you are sent off with the assurance that, once there, further help will be available. Although you make inquiries here and there as you go along, you cannot know the exact path that will take you to your final destination; nevertheless you are sure of arriving eventually because you are always able to find your way from place to place.

As students of spiritual science, we do not ask about the *ultimate* goal, but about the one lying immediately ahead—in other words, the goal of the Earth. We realize that it would be senseless to inquire about the ultimate goal, for we have recognized that evolution is a reality in human life. It must therefore never be forgotten that at the present stage of our existence it is not possible to understand the goals of much later phases of evolution and that a higher vantage point must be reached if we are to understand the meaning of a far distant goal. So we ask about the goal immediately ahead, realizing that by keeping it before us as an ideal and striving with the right means, we will eventually attain it, thereby reaching a further stage in development. At that stage it will be legitimate to ask about the *next* goal, and so on. Thus if it is ever suggested that spiritual science might tend to make people arrogant because the outlook extends beyond the ordinary world into a spiritual world, in reality their attitude will be one of humility toward these sublime matters about which superficial questions are so often asked.

We inquire, to begin with, about the goal of the Earth. In other words, what is it that human beings essentially add to the fruits of the preceding evolutionary periods of Saturn, Sun, and Moon by developing on the Earth through repeated physical incarnations? Here we will recall certain matters that will help us associate concrete and definite ideas with what may be called the "meaning and purpose" of Earth evolution. Let me speak to begin with of the following.

When intellectual thinking, based upon reason, came to birth during the Greco-Roman epoch (it would actually be true to say in the sixth century B.C.), a thought frequently uttered was that all philosophy, all deeper contemplation upon the secrets of existence, proceeds from wonder, from amazement. In other words, as long as human beings feel no wonder at the phenomena of life around them, their life is vapid and thoughtless, and they ask without intelligence about the why and wherefore of existence. "All philosophy begins with wonder" was a common saying during the ancient Greco-Roman epoch. What, in reality, does it signify in human soul-life?

It would be difficult today to find anyone in civilized Europe who has never set eyes on a locomotive in motion, but not so very long ago there were such persons; now, of course, they would be found only in very remote districts. If such people see a train moving along, they feel wonder and amazement at the sight of an object going forward without any of the familiar means. It is a known fact that many people, in their astonishment at seeing a locomotive in movement, asked if the horses pulling it were inside! Why were these people cast into amazement and wonder by what they saw? It was because they were looking at something that, in a certain sense, was known and unknown at the same time. They knew that things move forward, but whatever they had seen had always been provided with quite a different means of movement. Now they were looking at something they had never seen before. And this gives rise to wonder.

If people during the Greco-Roman epoch could become philosophers only when they were capable of wonder, they must have been people who perceived something at once known and unknown in everything taking place in the world, in that the happenings and phenomena seemed to contain more than appeared on the surface—something unknown. Why did the attitude of philosophers have to be that the primary causes and certain attributes of things in the world lay in a sphere unknown to them? Since it will be admitted that philosophers are at least as clever as people who give no thought at all to what goes on around them, it cannot be supposed that philosophers are capable of accepting only what is perceived by the ordinary senses. Therefore they must find something lacking, or rather they must surmise the presence of something that sets them wondering—something not present in the world of the senses. And so, before the days of materialism, philosophers always sought the supersensible in the phenomena presented to the senses. The wonder they felt is therefore associated with the fact that certain things are not to be comprehended through what presents itself to sensory eyes. They thought to themselves, What I perceive there does not tally with what I picture it to be; I must therefore conceive that supersensible forces are present within it. But the philosophers perceived no supersensible forces in the sense world. That alone is enough to make a thinking person realize that a subconscious memory, not reaching into consciousness, has persisted in the human being since times when the soul perceived something more than the actual phenomena of the sense world. In other words, remembrances arise of experiences undergone before the descent into sense existence. It is as if the soul were to say, I discern things and their effects that can invoke only wonder in me, because they are different from what I have seen before; enlightenment on them can be found only through forces that must be drawn from the supersensible world.

So all philosophizing begins with wonder, because in reality human beings approach the phenomena of existence as beings who come into the world of the senses from a supersensible world and find that the things of the sense world do not tally with what they perceived in the supersensible world. Wonder arises in them when sensible things are made manifest in a form that can be explained only by knowledge they once possessed in a supersensible world. Therefore wonder points to human beings' connection with the supersensible world, to something belonging to a sphere they can enter only when they transcend the world where the physical body encloses them. This is one indication of the fact that here, in this physical world, there is a continuous urge within human beings to reach out beyond themselves. A person who can simply remain shut up in the self, who is not driven by wonder beyond the field of the self, or ordinary ego, remains one who cannot reach beyond the self, who sees the Sun rise and set without a thought and with complete unconcern. This is the kind of existence led by uncivilized peoples.

A second power that releases human beings from the ordinary world, leading them at once away from purely material perception into supersensible insight, is compassion, fellow feeling (I have also spoken of this). Those who go heedlessly through the world do not regard compassion as having any great mystery about it; but to thoughtful people, compassion is a great and mysterious secret. When we look at a being only from outside, impressions come from it to our senses and intellect; with the awakening of compassion we pass beyond the sphere of these impressions. We share in what is taking place in its innermost nature; transcending the sphere of our own I, we pass over into its world. In other words, we are set free from ourselves; we break through the barriers of ordinary existence in the physical body and reach over into the other being. Here, already, is the supersensible—for neither the operations of the senses nor those of the reasoning mind can carry us into the sphere of another's soul. The fact that compassion exists in the world bears witness that even in the sense world we can be set free from, can pass beyond ourselves and enter the world of another being. People incapable of compassion contain a moral defect, a moral lack. If, at the moment they should get free from themselves and pass over into the other being to feel the pain or joy of the other, not their own—if at that moment their feelings fade and die away, then something is lacking in their moral life. Human beings on Earth, if they are to reach the stature of full and complete humanity, must be able to pass out beyond their own earthly life, must be able to live in another, not only in themselves.

Conscience is a third power whereby human beings transcend what they are in the physical body. In ordinary life they will desire this or that; according to their impulses or needs they will pursue what is pleasing to them and thrust aside what is displeasing. But in many such actions they will be their own critic, in that their conscience, the voice of their conscience, sounds a note of correction. Final satisfaction or dissatisfaction with what they have done also depends upon how the voice of conscience has spoken. This in itself is a proof that conscience is a power whereby human beings are led beyond the sphere of their impulses, their likes and dislikes.

Wonder and amazement, compassion or fellow feeling, conscience—these are the three powers through which human beings, even while in the physical body, transcend their own limitations; through these powers, influences that cannot find entrance into the human soul through the intellect and the senses ray into physical life.

It is easy to understand that these three powers can unfold only through incarnations in a body of flesh. Human beings must, as it were, be kept separate by a body of flesh from what pours into their life of soul from another sphere. If a body of flesh did not separate them from the spiritual world and present the outer world to them as a sense world, they would be incapable of wonder. It is the material body that enables wonder at the things of the sense world to arise in humans, compelling them to seek the Spirit. Compassion could not unfold if one human being were not separated from another, if people lived an undivided existence where a single flow of spiritual life pervaded the consciousness of all, if each soul were not separated from other souls by the impenetrable sheath provided by the physical body. And conscience could not be experienced as a spiritual force sending its voice into the world of natural human urges, passions, and desires, if the material body did not hanker after things that another power must warn against. And so human beings must be incarnated in physical bodies so that they may be able to experience wonder, compassion, and conscience.

In our time, people concern themselves little with such secrets, although they are profoundly enlightening. But in a past by no means very remote, a great deal of attention was given to these things. Just consider the world of the Greek gods, the gods of Homer; think of their actions and activities. Try to understand the nature of the impulses working in Achilles, a being who stands like a last survivor of an earlier generation on Earth. He too was born of a divine mother. Read through the *Iliad* and the *Odyssey* and ask yourselves whether this being, standing halfway between gods and men, was ever stirred by anything like conscience or compassion. Homer builds the whole of the *Iliad* around the fury of the wrath of Achilles—and wrath is a passion. Everything in the Greek legend centers around this; the *Iliad* tells of what came about as the result of a passion—the wrath of Achilles. Consider all the deeds of Achilles described in the *Iliad* and see if you can say of a single one that Achilles is moved by anything like compassion or conscience. Nor is there a single example of the stirring of wonder. The very greatness of Homer lies in his power to depict these things with such sublimity. When Achilles is told of some terrible happening, his behavior is far from that of a person filled with wonder. And then turn to the Greek gods themselves: they give vent to all kinds of impulses that are certainly egotistical when manifested in a human being enclosed in a physical body, but in the gods they are spiritual impulses. However, there is no compassion, no suggestion of conscience, nor anything like wonder in the Greek gods. Why not? Because Homer and the Greeks knew that these gods were beings belonging to a period of evolution preceding that of the Earth—a period when the beings then passing through their "human" stage under the prevailing conditions of existence had not yet received into the life of soul the powers of wonder, compassion, and conscience. It must be constantly remembered that the earlier planetary conditions the Earth passed through, where such beings as the Greek gods underwent their human stage, did not exist for the purpose of implanting wonder, compassion, and conscience in the life of soul. That is precisely the mission of Earth evolution! The purpose of Earth evolution is to implant into the evolutionary process as a whole powers that could otherwise never have come into existence: wonder, compassion, and conscience.

I have told you how the birth of conscience can be clearly traced to a certain period of Greek culture. In the works of Aeschylus, what we call conscience played no part; there were only remembrances of the avenging Furies. Not until we come to the works of Euripides is there any clear expression of conscience as we know it now. The concept of conscience arose only very gradually during the Greco-Roman epoch. I have told you that the concept of wonder arose for the first time when people began to philosophize in the world of Greco-Roman culture. And a remarkable fact in the spiritual evolution of Earth existence throws far-reaching light upon what we know as compassion, and also, in the true sense, love. In the age of materialism it is exceedingly difficult to maintain this concept of compassion or love in a true and right perspective. Many of you will realize that in our materialistic times this concept is distorted, in that materialism associates the concept of love so closely with sexuality—with which, fundamentally, it has nothing whatever to do. That is a point where the culture of our day abandons both intelligence and sound, healthy reason. Through its materialism, evolution in our time is veering not only toward the unintelligent and illogical but even toward the scandalous, when love is dragged into such close association with what is covered by the term *sexuality.* The fact that under certain circumstances the element of sexuality may be associated with love between man and woman is no argument for bringing the all-embracing nature of love or compassion so close together with the entirely specific character of sexuality. As far as logic is concerned, to associate the concept of, say, a railway engine with that of someone being run over, because engines do sometimes run over people, would be just about as intelligent as it is to connect the concept of love so closely with that of sexuality—simply because under certain circumstances there is an outward association. That this happens today is not the outcome of any scientific hypothesis but of the irrational and, to some extent, unhealthy mode of thinking prevailing in our time.

On the other hand, another telling fact points to the significance inherent in the concept of love and compassion. At a certain point in the evolution of humanity, something is made manifest among all peoples that, while differing in many essentials, is identical in one respect all over the Earth: the adoption of the concept of love, of compassion. It is very remarkable that six or seven centuries before the influx of the Christ impulse into humanity, founders of religions and systems of thought appeared all over the Earth, among all the peoples. It is of the highest significance that, six centuries before our era, Lao-tzu and Confucius should have been living in China, the Buddha in India, the last Zarathustra (not the original Zarathustra) in Persia, and Pythagoras in Greece. How great the differences are between these founders of religions! Only a mind abstracted from reality and incapable of discerning the differences can suggest, as is often mischievously done today, that the teachings of Lao-tzu or of Confucius do not differ from those of other founders of religions. Yet in one respect there is a similarity among them all; they all teach that compassion and love must reign between soul and soul! The significant point is this: six centuries before our era, consciousness begins to stir that love and compassion are to be received into the stream of human evolution. Thus whether we are thinking of the birth of wonder, of conscience, or of love and compassion in the stream of evolution ... all the signs point to the fact that in the fourth post-Atlantean cultural epoch, humankind was imbued with something that we may recognize as the "meaning and purpose" of Earth evolution.

It is so superficial and foolish when people ask why it was necessary for humankind to come down from the worlds of Divine Spirit into the physical world, only to have to reattain them. Why could it not have remained in the higher worlds? Humankind could not remain in those worlds because only by coming down into the physical world of Earth evolution could human beings receive into themselves the forces of wonder, love (or compassion), and conscience and moral obligation.

Looking at the fourth post-Atlantean cultural epoch, we perceive during its course the dawn of impulses that, in reality only from that time on, spread more and more widely among humankind. It is very easy today to emphasize how seldom humankind is ruled by compassion and love, how seldom by conscience. But in pointing to these things, we must also be mindful of the fact that in the Greco-Roman age slavery was still an accepted custom, and that even a philosopher as great as Aristotle still regarded the existence of slaves as a necessary principle of human life. We must also remember that since those days love has gained so much ground that even if inequalities still persist among people today, there is already present in their souls something like a feeling of shame that certain conditions exist. This in itself indicates that the forces that entered evolution at that time are unfolding within the souls of human beings. None would dare now, if they are to avoid the tragic fate of Nietzsche (the followers of Nietzsche can be ignored altogether, for in his right mind Nietzsche would have repudiated them), to stand openly for the introduction of slavery as it was in Greece. No one will deny that the greatest of all forces in the human soul is that of love and compassion, and that it must be humankind's task to make more and more articulate the voice that sounds out of another world into the soul.

Holding firmly in our minds that the unfolding of the three powers described constitutes the meaning and purpose of Earth evolution, we turn to the greatest of all impulses—the Christ impulse that poured into evolution during the fourth post-Atlantean epoch. Even outer circumstances indicate that this impulse was given at the very time when the Earth was ready for the development of the three powers of wonder, compassion or love, and conscience or moral obligation, as intrinsically human qualities. Many studies have given us a picture of how the Christ impulse made its way into the evolution of humankind.

I want here to refer to one aspect of the Christ impulse. I have told you that certain spiritual, superhuman forces were held back in the spiritual worlds at the beginning of the evolutionary process on the Earth. The Christ impulse flowed into the Earth at the time indicated in the Bible—that is, at the time of the Baptism in the Jordan. It was therefore an impulse untouched by the luciferic forces, since it had been kept back until the fourth post-Atlantean epoch; in that epoch it streamed into humanity....

If we conceive the Christ impulse to be the downpouring of the spiritual power that was kept back in the ancient Lemurian time in order to flow into evolution during the fourth post-Atlantean epoch at the point marked by the Baptism in the Jordan, reaching its culmination in the Mystery of Golgotha, then it is clear that the one known as the Christ was not, even then, incarnated in the ordinary sense in a physical human being. We know what complicated processes were connected with the man Jesus of Nazareth so that, for three years of his life, the Christ impulse might live within him. We are therefore able to understand that for three years the Christ impulse lived on the Earth in the three sheaths of a human being, but we also realize that even then the Christ impulse was not incarnated on the Earth in the ordinary sense, but that he pervaded the body of the being Jesus of Nazareth. This must be understood when it is said that it is not possible to speak of a *return* of Christ, but only of an *impulse* that was present once, during the time of the events in Palestine beginning with the Baptism in the Jordan, when only the physical body, the ether body, and the astral body of Jesus of Nazareth remained; within these sheaths the Christ was then present on the very soil of the Earth. From that time Christ has been united with the spiritual atmosphere of the Earth and can be found there by souls who are willing to receive him. From that time onward—and only from that time onward—he has been present in the spiritual atmosphere of the Earth. The great turn given to Earth evolution lies in the fact that from that time forward there was a power in the Earth that it did not previously contain.

We know that what we actually see in the kingdoms of nature around us is not reality, but *maya*, or great illusion. In the kingdom of the animals we see the individual forms coming into being and passing away; the group soul alone endures. In the plant kingdom, the individual plants appear and disappear, but behind them is the Earth spirit, which does not pass away. So it is, too, in the kingdom of the minerals. The spiritual endures, but the physical, whether in the animal, plant, or mineral kingdom, is transient, impermanent. Even the outer senses discern that the planet Earth is involved in a process of pulverization and will at some future time disintegrate into dust. We have spoken of how the Earth's body will be cast off by the spirit of the Earth, as the human body is cast off by the individual human spirit. What will remain as the highest substance of the Earth when its goal has been reached?

The Christ impulse was present on the Earth as "spiritual substance," so to speak. That impulse endures and will be received into human beings during the course of Earth evolution. But how does it live on? When the Christ impulse was upon the Earth for three years, it had no physical body, no ether body, no astral body of its own, but was enveloped in the three sheaths of Jesus of Nazareth. When the goal has been reached, the Earth, like the human being, will be a fully developed being, a meet and fitting vehicle for the Christ impulse. But where do the three sheaths of the Christ impulse originate? From forces that can be unfolded only on the Earth. Beginning with the Mystery of Golgotha, whatever has unfolded on the Earth since the fourth post-Atlantean period as the power of wonder, whatever comes to life in us as wonder, passes, finally, to the Christ, weaving the astral body of the Christ impulse. Love, or compassion, in the souls of human beings weaves the etheric body of the Christ impulse; and the power of conscience that, from the time of the Mystery of Golgotha until Earth's goal is attained, lives in and inspires human souls weaves the physical body (or what corresponds with the physical body) for the Christ impulse.

Only now can the true meaning of these words from the Gospel be discerned: "What you did for the least of my brothers, that you did for me" [Matt. 25:40]. The forces streaming from human being to human being are the units integrating the etheric body of Christ: love, or compassion, weaves the etheric body of Christ. Thus when the goal of Earth evolution is attained, he will be enveloped in the threefold vesture woven from the powers that have lived in human beings—powers that, when the limitations of the I have been transcended, become the sheaths of Christ.

And now think of how human beings live in communion with Christ. From the time of the Mystery of Golgotha until the attainment of the goal of Earth evolution, human beings grow more perfect in that they develop to the stature that is within their reach as a being endowed with the power of the I. But human beings are united with the Christ who has come among them when they transcend their own I—and, through wonder, build the astral body of Christ. Christ does not build his own astral body, but humans, in the wonder that arises in their souls, share in forming the astral body of Christ. His etheric body will be fashioned through the compassion and love flowing from person to person, and his "physical body" through the power of conscience unfolding in human beings. Whatever wrongs are committed in these three realms deprive the Christ of the possibility of full development on the Earth—that is to say, Earth evolution is left imperfect. Those who go about the Earth with indifference, who have no urge to understand what the Earth can reveal to them, deprive the astral body of Christ of the possibility of full development; those who live without unfolding compassion and love hinder the etheric body of Christ from full development; and those who lack conscience hinder the development of what corresponds with the physical body of Christ. And this means that the Earth cannot reach the goal of its evolution.

The principle of egotism has to be overcome in Earth's evolution. The Christ impulse penetrates more and more deeply into the life and culture of humankind, and the conviction that this impulse has lived its way into human beings free from every trace of denominationalism, as for example in the paintings of Raphael, will bear its fruit. How Christ may be truly portrayed is a problem still to be solved. Human beings on Earth will have to be greatly enriched in their life of feeling if another attempt, after the many made through the centuries, is to succeed to some slight extent in expressing what the Christ is as the supersensible impulse living on through Earth's evolution. The previous attempts do not even suggest what form such a portrayal of the Christ should take. It would have to express how the enveloping sheaths woven of the forces of wonder, compassion, and conscience are gradually made manifest. The countenance of Christ must be so vital and so alive that it expresses the victory over the sensory, desire nature in earthly humanity—victory achieved through the very forces that have spiritualized the countenance. There must be sublime power in this countenance.

In portraying the unusual form of a chin and mouth, painters or sculptors will have to express the power of conscience unfolded to its highest degree. The mouth must give the impression not that it is there to take in food, but to articulate whatever moral strength and power of conscience has been cultivated by humankind throughout the ages. The very structure of the bones around the teeth in the lower jaw will seem to take the form of a mouth. All this will have to be expressed in the countenance. The form of the lower part of the face will have to express a power whose outflowing rays seem to shatter the rest of the human body into pieces, changing that body so that certain other forces are vanquished.

With a mouth like this, it will be impossible to give the Christ figure a bodily form similar to that of the modern physical human being. On the other hand, all the power of compassion will flow from His eyes, the power that eyes alone can contain, not to receive impressions but to carry the soul itself into the joys and sufferings of others. His brow will not suggest thought based on earthly sense-impressions. It will be a brow that is conspicuous, prominent above the eyes, and arching over that part of the brain. It will not be the brow of a "thinker," which merely acts on the material already there. Wonder will be made to manifest in this projecting brow, which curves back gently over the head, expressing wonder and marvel at the world's mysteries. It will be the sort of head found nowhere in physical humanity.

Every true representation of the Christ must be a portrayal of the Ideal embodied in Him. When human beings reach out toward this highest ideal, striving by means of spiritual science to represent it in art, this feeling will arise in greater and greater strength: If you would portray the Christ, you must not look at what is actually there in the world but allow your whole being to be quickened and pervaded by all that flows from contemplating the world's spiritual evolution as inspired by the three great impulses of *wonder*, *compassion*, and *conscience*.

7.

The Buddha's Teaching of Compassion and Love

SEPTEMBER 25, 1909, BASEL

from *The Gospel of St. Luke*

YOU will have gathered from the lecture yesterday that a record like the Gospel of St. Luke cannot be understood unless the evolution of humankind is pictured from the higher vantage point of spiritual science—in other words, unless the transformations that have taken place in the whole nature and constitution of the human being during the process of evolution are kept in mind. In order to understand the radical change that came about in humankind at the time of Christ Jesus—and this is necessary for elucidation of the Gospel of St. Luke—it will be well to make a comparison with what is happening in our own age, admittedly less rapidly and more gradually, but for all that clearly perceptible to those possessed of insight.

To begin with we must entirely discard the frequently expressed idea, readily accepted by mental laziness, that nature, or evolution, makes no "jumps." In its ordinarily accepted sense, no statement could be more erroneous. Nature is perpetually making jumps! This very fact is essential and fundamental. Think, for example, of how the plant develops from the seed. The appearance of the first leaflet is evidence of an important jump. Another is made when the plant advances from leaf to flower, another when its life passes from the outer to the inner part of the blossom, and yet another, a very important one, when the fruit appears. Those who ignore the fact that such jumps occur very frequently will entirely fail to understand nature. When such people look at humankind and observe that development in some particular century proceeded at a snail's pace, they believe that the same will be the case during other periods. It may very well be that in a particular period development is slow, as it is in the plant from the first green leaf to the last. But just as a jump occurs in the plant when the last leaf has developed and the blossom appears, so do jumps continually occur in human evolution. The jump made when Christ Jesus appeared on Earth was so decisive that within a comparatively short time the old clairvoyance and the mastery of the spiritual over the bodily nature were so transformed that only remnants of clairvoyance and of the former power of the soul and spirit over the physical continued to exist. Hence, before that drastic change took place it was essential that whatever of the ancient heritage survived should once again be gathered together. It was in this milieu that Christ Jesus was to work. The new impulse could then be received into humankind and develop by slow degrees.

There is a leap occurring in another domain during our own epoch, but not as quickly. Although a longer period of time is involved, the parallel will be quite comprehensible to those who understand the character of the present age....

We are living in an age when it is becoming impossible for human hearts to accept the Bible as it has been accepted during the last four or five centuries of European civilization. Either people will receive spiritual science and through it learn to understand the Bible in a new way, or, as is now happening to many who are unacquainted with anthroposophy, they will cease to listen to the Bible. In that case they will lose the Bible altogether and with it untold spiritual treasures, actually the greatest and most significant spiritual treasures of our Earth evolution! This must be realized. We are now at the point where a jump is to take place in evolution; the human heart is demanding the spiritual scientific elucidation of the Bible. Given such elucidation, the Bible will be preserved, to the infinite blessing of humankind; without it the Bible will be lost. This should be taken earnestly by those who believe they must at all costs adhere to their personal inclinations and to the traditional attitude toward the Bible. Such, therefore, is the jump now being taken in evolution. Nothing will divert those who are aware of this from cultivating anthroposophy, because they recognize it as a necessity for the evolution of humankind.

Considered from a higher point of view, what is happening at the present time is relatively unimportant compared with what took place when Christ Jesus came to the Earth. In those days human evolution was at a stage where the last examples of its development since primeval times, actually since the previous embodiment of the Earth, still existed. Human beings were developing primarily in their physical, etheric, and astral bodies; the I had long since been membered into them but was still playing a subordinate role. Until the coming of Christ Jesus the fully self-aware I-being was still obscured by the three sheaths, the physical, etheric, and astral bodies.

Let us suppose that Christ Jesus had not come to the Earth. What would have happened? As evolution progressed the I would have emerged fully, but to the same extent that it emerged, all earlier outstanding faculties of the astral, etheric, and physical bodies, all the old clairvoyance, all the old mastery of the soul and the spirit over the body, would have vanished.

That would have been the inevitable course of evolution. The human being would have become a self-aware I-being, but the I would have led more and more to egoism and to the disappearance and extinction of love on the Earth. Human beings would have become I-beings, but utterly egotistical beings. That is the point of importance.

When Christ Jesus came to the Earth human beings were ready for the development of the Self, the I; for this very reason, however, they were beyond the stage where it would have been permissible to work upon them in the old way. In the ancient Hebrew period, for example, the Law, the proclamation from Sinai, was able to take effect because the I had not fully emerged and what the astral body, the highest part of the human constitution at that time, should do and feel in order to act rightly in the outer world was instilled, impressed into it. The Law of Sinai came to human beings as a last prophetic announcement in the epoch preceding the full emergence of the I. Had the I emerged and nothing else intervened, humans would have heeded nothing except their own I-being. Humankind was ready for the development of the I, but it would have been an empty I, concerned with itself alone and having no wish to do anything for others or for the world.

To give this I-being real substance, to so stimulate its development that the power of love would stream from it—that was the deed of Christ Jesus on the Earth. Without him the I would have become an empty vessel; through his coming it can become a vessel filled more and more completely with love. Christ could speak to those around him in this way: "When you see clouds gathering, you say there will be this or that weather; you judge what the weather will be by the outer signs, but the signs of the times you do not understand! If you were able to understand and assess what is going on around you, you would know that the Godhead must penetrate the I. Then you would not say, We can be satisfied with traditions handed down from earlier times. It is what comes from earlier times that is presented to you by the scribes and Pharisees, who wish to preserve the old and will allow nothing to be added to what was once given to humans. But that leaven will have no further effect in evolution. Those who say they will believe only in Moses and the Prophets do not understand the signs of the times, nor do they know what a transition is taking place in humanity" [see Luke 12:54–57].

In memorable words Christ Jesus told those around him that whether or not an individual will become a Christian does not depend upon personal inclination but upon the inevitable progress of evolution. By the words recorded in the Gospel of St. Luke about the "signs of the times," Christ Jesus wished to make it understood that the old leaven represented by the scribes and Pharisees, who preserved only what was antiquated, was no longer sufficient and that only those who felt no obligation to put aside personal inclinations and judge according to the necessity of the times could believe to the contrary. Hence Christ Jesus called what the scribes and Pharisees desired "Untruth"—something that does not tally with reality in the outer world. That would have been the real meaning of the expression.

We can best realize the forcefulness of these words by thinking of analogous happenings in our own day. How would we have to speak if we wished to apply to the present age what Christ Jesus said of the scribes and Pharisees? Are there, in our own times, any who resemble the scribes? Yes indeed! They are the people who will not accept the deeper explanation of the Gospels and refuse to listen to anything beyond the range of their own faculties of comprehension—faculties that have been unaffected by spiritual science; these people refuse to keep pace with the strides spiritual science has made in knowledge of the foundations of the Gospels. This is really everywhere the case when efforts, whether progressive or reactionary, are made to interpret the Gospels, for the fact is that the capacity for such interpretation can develop only in the soil of spiritual science. Spiritual science is the only source for deriving truth about the Gospels. That is why all other contemporary research seems so barren, so unsatisfactory, where there is a genuine desire to seek the truth.

Today, as well as "scribes and Pharisees," there are the natural scientists, a third type. We may therefore speak of three categories of people who want to exclude everything that leads to the spiritual, everything in the way of faculties attainable by human beings in order to penetrate to the spiritual foundations of the phenomena of nature. And those who, among others, must be impugned at the present time, if one speaks in the sense of true Christianity, are very often the holders of professorships! They have every opportunity for comparing and collating the phenomena of nature, but they entirely reject the spiritual explanations. It is they who hinder progress, for humankind's progress is hindered wherever there is refusal to recognize the signs of the times in the sense indicated.

In our days the only kind of action consistent with discipleship of Christ Jesus would be to find the courage to turn—as he turned against those who wished to confine truth to Moses and the Prophets—against people who retard progress by rejecting the anthroposophic interpretation of the Scriptures on the one side and the phenomena of nature on the other. Now and then there are really well-meaning people who occasionally would like to bring about a kind of vague reconciliation; it would be well if in the hearts of all such people there were some understanding of the words spoken by Christ Jesus as related in the Gospel of St. Luke.

Among the most beautiful and impressive parables in that Gospel is the one usually known as the parable of the unjust steward [Luke 16:1–13]. A rich man had a steward who was accused of wasting his goods. He therefore decided to dismiss the steward. The latter asked himself in dismay, "What will I do? I cannot support myself as a husbandman for I do not understand such work, nor can I beg, for I would be ashamed." Then the thought occurred to him: In all my dealings with the people with whom my stewardship brought me into contact, I had in mind only the interests of my lord; therefore they will have no particular liking for me. I have paid no attention to their interests. I must do something in order to be received into their houses and so not be utterly ruined; I will do something to show that I wish them well. Then he went to one of his lord's debtors and asked him, "How much do you owe?" And he allowed him to cancel half the debt. He did the same with the others. In this way he tried to ingratiate himself with the debtors, so that when his lord dismissed him he might be received by these people and not die of starvation. That was his object. The Gospel continues, possibly to the astonishment of some readers, "And the lord commended the unjust steward because he had done wisely." Those who set out to elucidate the Gospels today have actually speculated about which *lord* is meant, although it is absolutely clear that Jesus was praising the steward for his cleverness. Then the verse continues, "For the children of this world are in their generation wiser than the children of light." This is how the sentence has stood for centuries. But has anyone ever reflected upon what is meant by "the children of this world are in their generation wiser than the children of light?" "In their generation" is in all the different translations of the Bible. But if someone with only scanty knowledge were to translate the Greek text correctly, it would read, "For the children of this world in their way are wiser than the children of light"; that is, in their way the children of this world are wiser than the children of light, wiser according to their own understanding—that is what Christ meant. Translators of this passage have for centuries confused the expression "in their way" with a word that actually has a very similar sound in the Greek language; they have confused it, and do so to this very day, with *generations*, because the word was sometimes also used for the other concept. It hardly seems possible that this kind of thing should have dragged on for centuries and that modern, reputedly good translators, who have endeavored to convey the exact meaning of the text, should make no change. Weizsäcker, for example, gives this actual rendering! Strangely enough, people seem to forget the most elementary school-knowledge when they set about investigating biblical records. Spiritual science will have to restore the biblical records in their true form to the world, for the world today does not, properly speaking, possess the Bible and can have no real grasp of its contents. It might even be asked, Are these the genuine texts of the Bible? No, in very important parts they are not, as I will show you in still greater detail.

What is the meaning of this parable of the unjust steward? The steward thought, If I must leave my post I must gain the affection of the people. He realized that one cannot serve "two masters." Christ said to those around him, "You too must realize that you cannot serve two masters, the one who is now to enter human hearts as God and the one hitherto proclaimed by the scribes and the interpreters of the books of the Prophets. You cannot serve the God who is to draw into your souls as the Christ principle and give a mighty impetus to the evolution of humanity, and the other God who would hinder this evolution." Everything that was right and proper in a bygone age becomes a hindrance if carried over into a later stage of evolution. In a certain sense the process of evolution itself is based upon this principle. The powers that direct the "hindrances" were called at that time by the technical expression *Mammon.* "You cannot serve the God who will progress and Mammon, the god of hindrances. Think of the steward who, as a child of the world, realized that one cannot serve two masters, not even with the help of Mammon. So too should you perceive, in striving to become children of light, that you cannot serve two masters" [Luke 16:11–13].

Those living in the present age must also realize that no reconciliation is possible in our time between the god Mammon—the modern scribes and scientific pundits—and the direction of thought that must provide human beings with the nourishment they need. This is spoken in a truly Christian sense. Clothed in current language, what Christ Jesus wished to bring home to those around him in the parable of the unjust steward was that no one can serve two masters.

The Gospels must be understood in a really living way. Spiritual science itself must become a living reality! Under its influence everything it touches should be imbued with life. The Gospel itself should be something that streams into our own spiritual faculties. We should not just chatter about the scribes and Pharisees having been repudiated in the days of Christ Jesus, for then we would again be thinking only of a past age. We must know where the successor of the power described by Christ Jesus for his epoch as the god Mammon is to be found today. That is a living kind of understanding, and it is a very important factor in what is related in the Gospel of St. Luke. For with that parable, found only in this Gospel, is connected one of the most significant concepts in all the Gospels. It is a concept we can engrave into our hearts and souls only if we are able once again, and from a somewhat different angle, to make it clear how Buddha and the impulse he gave were related to Christ Jesus.

We have heard that Buddha brought to humankind the great teaching of compassion and love. Here is an instance where what is said in esotericism must be taken exactly as it stands; otherwise it might be objected that at one time Christ is said to have brought love to the Earth, and at another that Buddha brought the teaching of love. But is that the same? On one occasion I said that Buddha brought the *teaching* of love to the Earth and on another occasion that Christ brought love itself as a *living power* to the Earth. That is the great difference. Close attention is necessary when the deepest concerns of humankind are being considered; otherwise information given in one place is presented somewhere else in a quite different form, and then it is said that in order to be fair to everybody I have proclaimed two messengers of love! The very closest attention is essential in esotericism. When this enables us to really understand the words in which momentous truths are clothed, they are seen in the right light.

Knowing that the great teaching of compassion and love brought by Buddha is expressed in the Eightfold Path, we may ask ourselves, What is the aim of this Eightfold Path? What do humans attain when from the depths of their soul they adopt it as their life's ideal, never losing sight of the goal and asking continually, How can I reach the greatest perfection? How can I purify my I most completely? What must I do to enable my I to fulfil its function in the world as perfectly as possible? Such people will say to themselves: If I obey every precept of the Eightfold Path, my I will reach the greatest perfection it is possible to conceive. Everything is a matter of the purification and ennoblement of the I; everything that can stream from this wonderful Eightfold Path must penetrate into us. The important point is that it is work carried out by the I for its own perfecting. If, therefore, humans develop to further stages in themselves what Buddha set in motion as the "Wheel of the Law" (that is the technical term), their I-beings will gradually become possessed of wisdom at a high level—wisdom in the form of thought—and they will recognize the signs of perfection. Buddha brought the wisdom of love and compassion to humankind, and when we succeed in making the whole astral body a product of the Eightfold Path, we will possess the requisite knowledge of the laws expressed in its teachings.

But there is a difference between wisdom in the form of thought and wisdom as *living power*; there is a difference between knowing what the I must become and allowing the living power to flow into our very being so that it may stream forth again from the I into all the world as it streamed from Christ, working upon the astral, etheric, and physical bodies of those around him. The impulse given by the great Buddha enabled humankind to have knowledge of the teaching of compassion and love. What Christ brought is first and foremost a living power, not a teaching. He sacrificed his very Self. He descended in order to flow not merely into the astral bodies of human beings but into their I-beings, so that the I itself would have the power to ray out love as *substantiality.* Christ brought to the Earth the substantiality, the living essence of love, not merely the wisdom-filled content of love. That is the all-important point.

Nineteen centuries and roughly five more have now elapsed since the great Buddha lived on the Earth; in about three thousand years from now—this we learn from esotericism—a considerable number of human beings will have reached the stage of being able to evolve the wisdom of the Buddha, the Eightfold Path, out of their own moral nature, out of their own heart and soul. Buddha had once to be on Earth, and from him proceeded the power that humankind will develop little by little as the wisdom of the Eightfold Path. About three thousand years from now human beings will be able to unfold its teaching from within themselves; it will then be their own possession and they will no longer be obliged to receive it from outside. Then they will be able to say, This Eightfold Path springs from our very selves as the wisdom of compassion and love.

Even if nothing had happened other than the great Buddha's setting in motion the Wheel of the Law, humankind would have become capable of knowing the doctrine of compassion and love three thousand years from now. But it is a different matter to acquire also the faculty to embody it in very life. Not only to know about compassion and love, but, under the influence of an I-being, to unfold it as living—therein lies the difference. This faculty proceeded from Christ. He poured love itself into human beings, and it will grow from strength to strength. When humans have reached the end of their evolution, wisdom will have revealed to them the content of the doctrine of compassion and love; this they will owe to Buddha. But at the same time they will possess the faculty of letting the love stream out from the I over humankind; this they will owe to Christ.

Thus Buddha and Christ worked in cooperation, and the exposition given has been necessary so that the Gospel of St. Luke may be properly understood. We realize this at once when we know how to interpret correctly the words used in the Gospel [Luke 2:13–14]. The great proclamation is made to the shepherds. Above them is the "heavenly host"—this is the spiritual, imaginative expression for the Nirmanakaya of the Buddha.[1] What is it that is proclaimed to the shepherds from on high? The "manifestation (or revelation) of the wisdom-filled God from the Heights!" This is the proclamation made to the shepherds by the Nirmanakaya of Buddha, pictured as the "heavenly host" hovering over the Nathan Jesus-child. But something else is added: "And peace be to those on the Earth below who are filled with a good will"—that is, those in whom the living power of love is germinating. It is this that must gradually become reality on Earth through the new impulse given by Christ. To the "revelation from the Heights" he added the living *power*, bringing into every human heart and into every human soul something that can fill the soul to overflowing. He gave the human soul not merely a teaching that could be received in the form of thought and idea, but a power that can stream forth from it. The Christ-bestowed power that can fill the human soul to overflowing is called in the Gospel of St. Luke, and in the other Gospels also,

1. *Nirmanakaya* (literally, the "body that is built") refers, according to Theosophy, to the perfected human astral body as a state of being. "Nirmanakaya is [one who has become] a member of that invisible Host which ever protects and watches over humanity within Karmic limits." H.P. Blavatsky, *The Key to Theosophy* (Theosophical University Press, Wheaton, IL, 1991, glossary). As meant here, Buddhists would be more likely to use the term *Sambhokakaya* (the subtle, imagination body), since Nirmanakaya is considered to be the physical manifestation of the Buddha.

the power of *faith*. This is what the Gospels mean by faith. Those who receive Christ into themselves so that Christ lives in them, whose I-being is not an empty vessel but is filled to overflowing with love—such people have faith.

Why could Christ be the supreme illustration of the power of "healing through the word"? Because he was the first to set in motion the "Wheel of Love" (not the "Wheel of the Law") as a freely working faculty and power of the human soul; because love in the very highest measure was within him—love brimming over in such abundance that it could pour into those around him who needed to be healed; because the words he spoke, no matter whether "Stand up and walk!" or "Your sins are forgiven," or other words, issued from overflowing love. His words were uttered from overflowing love, love transcending the limits of the I. And those who were able to some extent to experience this were called by Christ "the faithful." This is the only true interpretation of the concept of faith—one of the most fundamental concepts in the New Testament. Faith is the capacity to transcend the self, to transcend what the I can, for the time being, achieve.

Therefore when he had passed into the body of the Nathan Jesus and had there united with the power of the Buddha, Christ's teaching was not concerned with the question, "How shall the I achieve the greatest possible perfection?" but rather with the question, "How shall the I overflow? How can the I transcend its own limits?" He often used simple words, and indeed the Gospel of St. Luke as a whole speaks to the hearts of the simplest people. Christ said, in effect: It is not enough to give something only to those who you know for certain will give it back to you again, for sinners also do that. If you know that it will come back to you, your action has not been prompted by overflowing love. But if you give something knowing that it will not come back to you, then you have acted out of pure love, for pure love is what the I does not keep enclosed but releases as a power that flows forth from a person [Luke 6:33–35]. In many and various ways Christ speaks of how the I must overflow and how the power overflowing from the I, and from feeling emancipated from self-interest, must work in the world.

The words of greatest warmth in the Gospel of St. Luke are those telling of this overflowing love. The Gospel itself will be found to contain this overflowing love if we let its words work upon us in such a way that the love pervades all our own words, enabling them to make their effect in the outer world. Another Evangelist, who because of his different antecedents puts less emphasis upon this particular secret of Christianity, has for all that summarized it in a short sentence. In the Latin translation of the Gospel of St. Matthew we still have the genuine, original words that epitomize the many beautiful passages about love in the Gospel of St. Luke: *Ex abundantia cordis os loquitur.* "Out of the abundance of the heart the mouth speaks" [Matt. 12:34]. This expresses one of the very highest Christian ideals! The mouth speaks from the overflowing heart, from what the heart does not confine within itself. The heart is set in motion by the blood, and the blood is the expression of the I. The meaning is therefore this: "Speak from an I that overflows and rays out power (the power of faith). Then will your words contain the power of Christ!" "Out of the abundance of the heart the mouth speaks!"—this is a cardinal principle of Christianity.

In the modern German Bible this passage is rendered, "His mouth overflows whose heart is full."[2] These words have for centuries succeeded in obscuring a cardinal principle of Christianity. The absurdity of saying that the heart overflows when it is "full" has not dawned upon people, although things do not generally overflow unless they are *more* than full! Humankind—this is not meant as criticism—has inevitably become entangled in an idea that obscures an essential principle of Christianity and has never noticed that the sentence as it stands here is meaningless. If it is contended that the German language does not allow a literal translation of *Ex abundantia cordis os loquitur* into "Out of the abundance of the heart the mouth speaks," on the ground that one cannot say "The abundance of the stove makes the room warm"—that too is senseless. For if the stove is heated only to the extent that the warmth just reaches its sides, the room will not be heated; it will be heated only when a superabundance of warmth comes out of the stove. Here we light upon a very significant point: a cardinal principle of Christianity, one upon which part of the Gospel of St. Luke is based, has been entirely obscured, with the result that the meaning of one of the most important passages in the Gospel has remained hidden from humanity.

The power that can overflow from the human heart is the Christ power. *Heart* and *I* are here synonymous. What the I is able to create when transcending its own limits flows forth through the word. Not until the end of Earth evolution will the I be fit to enshrine the nature of Christ in its fullness. In the present age Christ is a power that brims over from the heart. Those who are content that their heart shall merely be *full* do not possess the Christ. Hence an essential principle of Christianity is obscured if the weight and significance of this sentence are not realized. Things of infinite importance, belonging to the

2. See Matthew 12:34 and Luke 6:45. The correct meaning has been preserved in the English versions.

very essence of Christianity, will come to light through spiritual science's elucidation of the sacred records of Christianity. By reading the Akashic Chronicle, spiritual science is able to discover the original meanings and thus to read the records in their true form.

We can now understand how humanity advances into the future. The Bodhisattva who became Buddha five or six centuries before our era ascended into the spiritual world and now works in his Nirmanakaya. He has risen to a higher stage and need not again descend into a physical body. The powers that were his as Bodhisattva are again present—but in a different form. When he became Buddha at that time, he passed over the office of Bodhisattva to another who became his successor; another became Bodhisattva. A Buddhist legend speaks of this in words that express a deep truth of Christianity. It is narrated that the Bodhisattva, before descending to the incarnation when he became Buddha, removed his heavenly tiara and placed it upon the Bodhisattva who was to be his successor. The latter, with his somewhat different mission, works on. He too is to become a Buddha. When, in about three thousand years, a number of human beings have evolved from within themselves the teachings of the Eightfold Path, the present Bodhisattva will become Buddha, as did his predecessor. Entrusted with his mission five or six centuries before our era, he will become Buddha in about three thousand years, reckoning from our present time. Oriental wisdom knows him as the Maitreya Buddha.[3]

3. There are countless references to the Maitreya Buddha in Buddhist literature: see "Maitreya, the future Buddha," in *Buddhist Scriptures* (trans. Edward Conze, Penguin Classics, New York, 1959). For Steiner's understanding of the Buddha's relationship to the Christ, see *From Buddha to Christ* (Anthroposophic Press, Hudson, NY, 1987).

Before the present Bodhisattva can become the Maitreya Buddha a considerable number of human beings must have developed the precepts of the Eightfold Path out of their own hearts, and by that time many will have become capable of this. Then he who is now the Bodhisattva will bring a new power into the world.

If nothing further were to have happened by then, the future Buddha would, it is true, find human beings capable of thinking out the teachings of the Eightfold Path through deep meditation, but he would not find ones having within their inmost soul the living, overflowing power of love. This living power of love must stream into humankind in the intervening time so that the Maitreya Buddha will find not only human beings who understand what love is, but also those who have within them the power of love. It was for this purpose that Christ descended to the Earth. He descended for three years only, never having been embodied on the Earth before, as you will have gathered from everything that has been said. The presence of Christ on the Earth for three years, from the Baptism by John until the Mystery of Golgotha, meant that love will flow in ever increasing measure into the human heart, into the human soul—in other words, into the human I—so that at the end of Earth evolution the I will be filled with the power of Christ. Just as the teaching of compassion and love had first to be kindled to life through the Bodhisattva, the *substance* of love had to be brought down from heavenly heights to the Earth by the Being who allows it gradually to become the possession of the human I itself. We may not say that love was not previously in existence. What was not present before the coming of Christ was the love that could be the direct possession of the human I; it was inspired love that Christ enabled to stream down from cosmic heights; it streamed into human beings unconsciously, just as previously the Bodhisattva had enabled the teaching of the Eightfold Path to stream into them unconsciously. Buddha's relation to the Eightfold Path was analogous to the status of the Christ Being before it was possible for him to descend to take human form. Taking human form signified progress for Christ. That is the all-important point. Buddha's successor, now a Bodhisattva, is well known to those versed in spiritual science, and the time will come when these facts—including the name of the Bodhisattva who will then become the Maitreya Buddha—will be spoken of explicitly. For the present, however, when so many factors unknown to the external world have been presented, indications must suffice. When this Bodhisattva appears on Earth and becomes the Maitreya Buddha, he will find on Earth the seed of Christ, embodied in those human beings who say: "Not only is my head filled with the wisdom of the Eightfold Path; I have not only the teaching, the wisdom of love, but my heart is filled with the living substance of love which overflows and streams into the world." And then, together with such human beings, the Maitreya Buddha will be able to carry out his further mission in the world's evolution.

All these truths are interrelated, and only by realizing this are we able to understand the profundities of the Gospel of St. Luke. This Gospel does not speak to us of a "teaching," but of the one who flowed as very substance into the beings of the Earth and into the constitution of human beings. This is a truth expressed in esotericism by saying: The Bodhisattvas who become Buddhas can, through wisdom, redeem earthly human beings in respect to the spirit, but they can never redeem the whole human being. For the whole human being can be redeemed only when the warm power of love, and not wisdom alone, flows through the whole being. The redemption of souls through the outpouring of love that He brought to the Earth—that was the mission of Christ. The mission of the Bodhisattva and of the Buddha was to bring the wisdom of love; the mission of Christ was to bring to humankind the power of love. This distinction must be made.

8.

Faith, Love, Hope

I

DECEMBER 2, 1911, NUREMBERG

from *Faith, Love, Hope*

THIS evening and tomorrow evening we shall attempt a coherent study of the nature of the human being and the human connection with the esoteric foundations of the present time and the near future. From various indications I have given here you will have grasped that today we are, to some extent, facing a new revelation, a new announcement to humankind. If we keep in mind the recent periods of human evolution, it may well be that we will best understand what is approaching if we connect it with two other important revelations. In doing so we will be considering, it is true, only what has been revealed to humankind in times relatively near our own.

These three revelations—the one now to come and the two others—may be best understood by comparing them to the early development of a child. By observing children properly, we find that when they first come into the world they must be protected and cared for by those around them; they have no way to express what is going on within them or to formulate in thought what affects their souls. To begin with, children cannot speak or think; everything must be done for them by those who have received them in their midst. Then they begin to speak.

Those who watch attentively—this is mentioned in my book *The Education of the Child*[1]—know that first children imitate what they hear, and that during the early days of speaking they have no understanding that can be attributed to thinking. What they say does not arise from thought. Precisely the opposite happens; they learn to think by talking and learn gradually to apprehend in clear thought what they were previously prompted to say from the hidden depths of feeling.

Thus, we have three successive periods in child development: first, a period when children are unable to speak or think; second, a period when they can speak but not yet think; and third, a period when they become conscious of thoughts in what they say. We may compare these three stages in the child's development with what humankind has gone through—and has still to go through—since about fifteen hundred years before the Christian era.

The first revelation that we may speak of as coming to humankind during the present cycle of time is the revelation proceeding from Sinai as the Ten Commandments. Anyone going more deeply into the significance of what was revealed to humankind in these commandments will find great cause for wonder. The fact is, however, that people take these spiritual treasures so much for granted that little thought is given to them. But those who reflect upon their significance have to admit how remarkable it is that in these Ten Commandments something is given that has spread through the world as law, something that in its fundamental character still holds good today and forms the basis of the law in all countries, insofar as,

1. *The Education of the Child and Early Lectures on Education*, Anthroposophic Press, Hudson, NY, 1996.

during the last thousand years, the Ten Commandments have gradually been adopted by modern civilization. Something all-embracing, grand, universal, is revealed to humankind as if in these words: There is a primal Being in the spiritual world whose image is here on Earth—the I. This Being can so infuse his own power into the human I, so pour himself into it, that a person is enabled to conform to the norms, the laws, given in the Ten Commandments.

The second revelation came about through the Mystery of Golotha. What can we say about this Mystery? What can be said was indicated yesterday in the public lecture "From Jesus to Christ." It was shown there that just as we can only understand human beings in their bodily nature as descending through the generations from the original human couple on Earth, so we can only understand rightly the greatest gift coming to our I-being—which must sink more and more into our I-being during earthly existence—by tracing it back to the Mystery of Golgotha. It need not concern us here that the old Hebrew tradition has a different conception from that of present-day science. If we trace back human beings' blood relationship, their bodily relation, to that original human couple, Adam and Eve, who once lived on Earth as the first physical personalities, the primal forebears of humankind, and if we must therefore say that the blood flowing in human veins goes back to that human pair, we can ask: Where must we look for the origin of the most precious gift bestowed on our soul, that holiest, most valuable gift, which accomplishes never-ending marvels in the soul and makes itself known to our consciousness as something higher than the ordinary I within us? For the answer we must turn to what arose from the grave on Golgotha. What arose then lives on in every human soul that has experienced an inner awakening, just as the blood of Adam and Eve continues to live in the body of every human being. We have to see a kind of fountainhead, a primal fatherhood, in the risen Christ—the spiritual Adam who enters the souls of those who have experienced an awakening, bringing them for the first time to the fullness of their I, to what gives life to their I in the right way. Thus, just as the life of Adam's body lives on in the physical bodies of all human beings, what arose from the grave on Golgotha flows in like manner through the souls of those who find the path to it. That is the second revelation given to humankind; we are enabled to learn what happened through the Mystery of Golgotha.

If in the Ten Commandments human beings have received guidance from outside, this guidance may be compared to what happens to the child before it can either speak or think. What is done for the child by its environment was achieved by the old Jewish law for all humankind, which until then lacked, as it were, the power of speaking and thinking. Human beings, however, have now learned to speak—or, rather, have learned something that may be compared with a child's learning to speak: they have gained knowledge of the Mystery of Golgotha through the Gospels. And the way they first understood the Gospels may be compared with how a child learns to speak. Through the Gospels there has come to human souls and human hearts some degree of understanding for the Mystery of Golgotha, which finds its way into human feelings and perceptions, and into the soul forces arising in us when, for example, we allow the deeply significant, intuitive scenes and pictures drawn from the Gospels by great painters to work upon us. It is the same with traditional pictures of the adoration of the child by the Shepherds or by the Wise Men from the East, of the flight into Egypt, and so on. All this leads back in the end to the Gospels; it has reached human understanding in such a way that humans may be said to have learned to speak, in their fashion, about the Mystery of Golgotha. In this connection we are now moving toward the third period, which may be compared with how the child learns the thought content in its own speech and can become conscious of it. We are approaching the revelation that should give us the full content, the thought content, of the Gospels—all that they contain of soul and spirit. For at present people understand the Gospels no better than the child understands what it says before it can think. In the context of world history, people are meant to learn through spiritual science to reflect upon the thoughts in the Gospels, to let the whole deep spiritual content of the Gospels work upon them for the first time. This indeed is connected with a further great event that humankind can feel approaching and will experience before the end of the twentieth century. This event can be brought before our souls in somewhat the following way: If once again we enter the nature of the Mystery of Golgotha, we realize that the elements of the Christ that rose from the grave of Golgotha have remained with the Earth, so that they can directly affect every human soul, awakening the I to a higher stage of existence. We may say that through the Mystery of Golgotha Christ became the Spirit of the Earth and has remained so since that time. In our day, however, a change is coming in the relation of the Christ to human beings, an important change you have come to know something about—the new revelation of the Christ to human beings.

This revelation can also be characterized in another way. To do this we must turn to what happens when human beings go through the gate of death. (This is something that could not be described in books, but must now be spoken of.) When human beings have passed through the gate of death, have experienced the backward survey of the previous earthly life, and have come to the point when the etheric body is laid aside and the time has come for kamaloka, they are first met by two figures. Usually only one is mentioned, but to complete the picture—and this is a reality for every true esotericist—we must say that before kamaloka the human being is confronted by two figures. What I am now telling you holds good, it is true, only for people of the West and for those who, during the last one thousand years, have been connected with Western culture. These people are confronted after death by two figures. One is Moses—they know quite clearly that it is Moses who stands before them, holding out the tables of the law. In the Middle Ages Moses "with his stern law" was spoken of. And in their souls human beings are keenly aware of how far in their inmost being they have transgressed against this law. The other figure is "the Cherubim with the flaming sword," who pronounces judgment on these transgressions. That is an experience human beings have after death. Thus, in accordance with spiritual science, it can be said that there is a kind of settlement of the karmic account by these two figures—Moses with the stern law and the Cherubim with the flaming sword.

In our time, however, a change is approaching, an important change that can be described in this way. Christ is becoming Lord of Karma for all those who, after death, experience what has just been discussed. Christ is entering his judgeship. Let us look more closely into this fact. From the world conception of spiritual science, we all know that a karmic account is kept of our life; that there is a certain balancing of the deeds standing on the credit side of the account—the sensible deeds, the fine deeds, those that are good—and, on the other side, the bad, ugly, lying deeds and thoughts.

Now it is important, on the one hand, that in the further course of their earthly lives individuals should themselves adjust the balance of this karmic account. But this living out of the result of good and splendid deeds, or of those that are bad, can be done in many different ways. The particular adjustment in the future life is not always determined after the same pattern. Suppose someone has done a bad action; that person must compensate for it by doing a good one. This good action, however, can be achieved in two ways, and it may require the same effort on the person's part to do good to a few people only as to benefit a considerable number. The concern of the Christ, who in our time is becoming Lord of Karma, will be to ensure that in the future, when we have found our way to him, our karmic accounts will be balanced—inserted in the cosmic order—in a way that will benefit as many people as possible.

This taking over by Christ of the judging of a person's actions is a result of his direct intervention in human destiny. This intervention is not in a physical body; it is on behalf of those human beings on Earth who will increasingly acquire the capacity to perceive him. There will be people, for instance, who suddenly become aware of an urge to refrain from doing something they are doing, because of a remarkable vision. They will perceive in a dreamlike way what appears to be their own action, yet they will not be able to remember having done it. There will be more and more cases of this from now on during the next three thousand years.

Those who, in the course of their evolution, are not prepared for such a thing to happen will look upon it as merely imagination run wild or as a pathological condition of the soul. However, those who, through spiritual science, have been sufficiently prepared for the revelation being renewed for humanity in our time—this third revelation during the most recent cycle of humanity—will understand that this all points to the development of new human faculties, ones that enable human beings to see into the spiritual world. They will also realize that the image appearing to their soul is a forewarning of the karmic act that must be accomplished—either in this earthly life or in a later one—to compensate for what they have done. In other words, people will gradually achieve, through their own efforts, the faculty for perceiving in a vision the karmic adjustment, the compensating deed, that must be accomplished in the future. From this fact it can be seen that in our time as well we should say, as did John the Baptist by the Jordan, Change your state of soul, for the time is coming when new faculties will awake in human beings.

But this form of karmic perception will arise in such a way that here and there the figure of the etheric Christ—the actual Christ as he is living in the astral world—will be directly visible to some individual, not in the physical body, but as the newly awakened human faculties he will manifest on Earth as counsellor and protector of those who need advice, help, or solace in the loneliness of their lives.

The time is coming when human beings who feel depressed and miserable for one reason or another will increasingly find the help of their fellows less important and valuable. The force of individuality, of individual life, will count for more and more, while the power of one person to work helpfully upon the soul of another, which held good in the past, will tend constantly to diminish. In its stead the great Counsellor will appear, in etheric form.

Therefore the best advice we can receive for the future (and this certainly applies to young people today) is to strengthen our souls and fill them with energy; in this way, as we advance into the future (whether in this incarnation or in the next), we may realize with increasing strength the newly awakened faculties that give us knowledge of the great Counsellor, who at the same time is becoming the judge of a person's karma. This is knowledge of Christ in his new form. For those who have already prepared here for the Christ event of the twentieth century, when this event becomes widely experienced it will make no difference whether they are in the physical body or have passed through the gate of death; those who have passed through will still correctly understand the Christ event and have the right connection with it. This will not be the case, however, for those who have thoughtlessly passed by this third great forewarning given to humanity through spiritual science. The Christ event must be prepared for in the physical body here on Earth. Those who go through the gate of death without giving even a glance into spiritual science during their present incarnation will have to wait until their next incarnation before gaining a right understanding of the Christ event. It is an actual fact that those who have never heard on the physical plane of the Christ event are unable to come to an understanding of it between death and rebirth. They too must wait until they can prepare for it upon their return to the physical plane. Therefore, when their present incarnations end at death, these people in their essential being remain unconcerned in the face of the mighty event referred to—Christ's assuming the judgeship, the possibility of his intervening, in an etheric body, directly from the astral world in the evolution of humankind, and his becoming visible in various places.

It is characteristic of human evolution that old human attributes not closely connected with spiritual evolution gradually lose significance. When we consider human evolution since the Atlantean catastrophe, we can say that among the great differentiations prepared during the Atlantean age, present-day human beings have become accustomed to those of race. We can still speak in a certain sense of an old Indian race, of an old Persian race, of an Egyptian or a Greco-Latin one, and even of something in our own time corresponding to a fifth race. But the concept of race in relation to human evolution is ceasing to have a right meaning. In the sixth cultural epoch, which will follow our own, something that applied in earlier times will no longer apply—the necessity of having some spatial center to spread the culture of the epoch. The important thing is the spreading of spiritual science among people without distinction of race, nation, or family. In the sixth cultural epoch those who have accepted spiritual science will come out of every race and will found, throughout the Earth, a new culture no longer based on the concept of race; that concept will have lost its significance. In short, what is important in the world of maya, the external world of space, vanishes; we must learn to recognize this in the future course of our spiritual science movement.

At the beginning this was not understood. Therefore, when we read Olcott's *Buddhist Catechism*, which once served well, we get the impression that races continue to roll on like so many wheels. But for the coming time, such concepts are losing their significance. Everything subject to the limitations of space will lose significance. Anyone, therefore, who thoroughly understands the meaning of human evolution understands that the coming appearance of Christ during the next three thousand years does not involve the restriction of Christ to a body limited by space nor to a certain territory. Neither will his appearance be limited to one place at a time. His help will arrive at the same moment here, there, and everywhere. A spiritual being is not subject to the laws of space, and anyone who can be helped by Christ's direct presence is able to receive that help at one end of the Earth just as well as someone at the opposite end. Only those who are unwilling to recognize humanity's progress toward spirituality and what gradually transforms all the most important events into the spiritual can declare that the Being of Christ implies a limitation to the physical body.

We have now described the facts concerning the third revelation and how this revelation is already in the process of throwing new light on the Gospels. The Gospels are the language, and anthroposophy is their thought content. As language is related to a child's full consciousness, so are the Gospels related to the new revelation that comes directly from the spiritual world—related, in effect, to what spiritual science is to become for humankind. When we come to discern, first out of the soul's unconscious depths and then ever more clearly, our connection with anthroposophy, we must be aware that we have in fact a certain task to fulfil, a task of understanding,.

We must look upon it, in a sense, as a mark of distinction bestowed by the World Spirit, a sign of grace on the part of the creative guiding spirit of the world, when today our heart urges us toward this new announcement that is added, as a third revelation, to those proclaimed from Sinai and from the Jordan. The task given in this new announcement is to learn to know the human being in its entire being—to perceive ever more deeply that what we are principally conscious of is sheathed in other members of the human being, which are nevertheless important for a person's life as a whole.

*

It is necessary for our friends to learn about these matters from the most varied points of view. So I will now say a few words about the human being's inner being. You know that if we start from the actual center of its being, from the I, we come next to the sheath we give the more or less abstract name of astral body. Further out we find the so-called etheric body, and still further outside, the physical body. From the point of view of real life we can speak about the human sheaths in another way, and today we will take directly from life what can, it is true, be learned only from esoteric insight, but can be understood through unprejudiced observation.

Many people, due to their so-called scientific world conception, have become arrogant and overbearing, and say, "The ages of faith are long gone; they were suited to humanity during its childhood phase, but now we have progressed to knowledge. People must have knowledge of everything today and should no longer merely believe." Now that may all sound very good, but it is not based on genuine understanding. We must ask more than simply whether knowledge has been gained through ordinary science during current human evolution. Other questions must be asked: Is faith itself significant for humanity? Isn't it part of a person's very nature to believe?

Of course, it might be possible for some to want to dispense with faith, for some reason, and throw it away. People can, for awhile, play fast and loose with their health without any obvious harm; when they come to view faith as merely a cherished gift to their ancestors in the past, it is the same as recklessly abusing one's health for awhile and, in this way, depleting the forces one possessed previously. When people view faith in that way, they are still—as far as the life forces of their soul are concerned—living on the old gift of faith handed down to them through tradition. It is not for human beings to decide whether to lay aside faith or not; faith is a question of life-giving forces in the soul. The important point is not whether we believe or not, but that the forces expressed in the word *faith* are necessary to the soul. For the soul incapable of faith becomes withered, dried up like the desert.

There were once human beings who, without any knowledge of natural science, were much more clever than those today with a scientific world conception. They did not say, as people imagine they would have said, "I believe what I do not know." They said, "I believe what I know for certain." Knowledge is the only foundation of faith. We should know in order to take increasing possession of the forces that are the forces of faith in the human soul. In our soul we must have what enables us to look toward a supersensible world, what makes it possible for us to turn all our thoughts and conceptions in that direction.

If we do not possess forces like those expressed in the word *faith*, something in us goes to waste; we wither like leaves in autumn. For a while this may not seem to matter, but then things begin to go wrong. Were human beings in reality to lose all faith, they would soon see what it means for evolution. By losing the forces of faith they would be incapacitated for finding their way about in life; their very existence would be undermined by fear, care, and anxiety. To put it briefly, it is only through the forces of faith that we can receive the life that should well up to invigorate the soul. This is because, imperceptible at first for ordinary consciousness, something lies in the hidden depths of our being in which our true I is embedded. This something, which immediately makes itself felt if we fail to bring it fresh life, is the human sheath where the forces of faith are active. We may term it the *faith soul,* or, as I prefer, the *faith body.* It has hitherto been given the more abstract name of astral body. The most important forces of the astral body are those of faith, so the term astral body and the term faith body are equally justified.

A second force that is also to be found in the hidden depths of a person's being is the force expressed by the word *love.* Love is not only something that links human beings together; it is also needed by them as individuals, When people are incapable of developing the force of love, they become dried up and withered in their inner being. We have merely to picture to ourselves those who are such great egoists that they are unable to love. Even where the case is less extreme, it is sad to see people who find it difficult to love, who pass through an incarnation without the living warmth that love alone can generate—love for something on Earth, at any rate.

Such persons are a distressing sight as they go through the world in their dull, prosaic way. Love is a living force that stimulates something deep in our being, keeping it awake and alive—an even deeper force than faith. And just as we are cradled in a body of faith, which from another aspect can be called the astral body, so are we cradled also in a body of love, or, as we call it in spiritual science, the etheric body, the body of life forces. For the chief forces working in us from the etheric body, out of the depths of our being, are those expressed in the human capacity for loving at every stage of our existence. What if people could completely empty their being of the force of love—but, in fact, that is impossible for the greatest egoist, thank God; for even in egoistic striving there is still an element of love. For example: those who are unable to love anything else can often begin, if sufficiently avaricious, by loving money—at least substituting another love for charitable love, though it arises from egoism. If there were no love at all in a human being, the enveloping structure that should be sustained by love forces would shrivel, and the person, empty of love, would actually perish; such a person would in fact die physically.

This withering of love's forces can also be called a withering of the etheric body's forces, for the etheric body is the same as the body of love. Thus at the very center of a human being we have its essential kernel, the I, surrounded by its enveloping structures: first the body of faith, and then the body of love around it.

If we go farther, we come to another set of forces we all need in life, and if some people do not, or cannot, have them at all, that is very distinctly to be seen in their external nature. For the forces we need emphatically as life-giving forces are those of hope, of confidence in the future. As far as the physical world is concerned, people cannot take a single step in life without hope. They certainly make strange excuses sometimes, if they are unwilling to acknowledge that human beings need to know something of what happens between death and rebirth. They say, "Why do we need to know that, when we don't know what will happen to us here from one day to another? So why are we supposed to know what takes place between death and a new birth?" But do we actually know nothing about tomorrow? We may have no knowledge of what is important for the details of our supersensible life, or, to speak more bluntly, whether or not we will be physically alive. But we do know one thing—that if we are physically alive tomorrow there will be morning, mid-day, evening, just as there are today. If as a carpenter I make a table today, it will still be there tomorrow; if I am a shoemaker, someone will be able to put on tomorrow what I make today; and if I sow seeds I know that next year they will come up. We know about the future just as much as we need to know. Life would be impossible in the physical world were not future events to be preceded by hope in this rhythmical way. Would anyone make a table today without being sure it would not be destroyed in the night; would anyone sow seeds without having an idea about what would become of them?

It is precisely in physical life that we need hope, for everything is upheld by hope and without it nothing can be done. The forces of hope, therefore, are connected with our last sheath as human beings, with our physical body. What the forces of faith are for our astral body and the love forces are for the etheric body, the forces of hope are for the physical body. Thus people who are unable to hope, who are always despondent about what they suppose the future may bring, will go through the world with this clearly visible in their physical appearance. Nothing makes for deep wrinkles, those deadening forces in the physical body, sooner than lack of hope.

The inmost kernel of our being may be said to be sheathed in our faith body or astral body, in our body of love or etheric body, and in our hope body or physical body. We comprehend the true significance of our physical body only when we bear in mind that, in reality, it is not sustained by external physical forces of attraction and repulsion—that is a materialistic idea—but has in it what, according to our concepts, we know as forces of hope. Our physical body is built up by hope, not by forces of attraction and repulsion. This very point can show that the new spiritual scientific revelation gives us the truth.

What then does spiritual science give us? By revealing the all-embracing laws of karma and reincarnation, spiritual science gives us something that permeates us with spiritual hope, just as does our awareness on the physical plane that the Sun will rise tomorrow and that seeds will eventually grow into plants. It shows, if we understand karma, that our physical body, which will perish into dust when we have gone through the gate of death, can through the forces permeating us with hope be rebuilt for a new life. Spiritual science fills people with the strongest forces of hope. Were this spiritual science, this new revelation for the present time, to be rejected, human beings naturally would return to Earth in future all the same, for life on Earth would not cease because of people's ignorance of its laws. Human beings would incarnate again; but there would be something very strange about these incarnations. Human beings would gradually become a race with bodies wrinkled and shrivelled all over, earthly bodies that would finally be so crippled that people would be entirely incapacitated. To put it briefly, in future incarnations a condition of dying away, of withering up, would assail human beings if their consciousness, and from there the hidden depths of their being right down into the physical body, were not given fresh life through the power of hope.

This power of hope arises through the certainty of knowledge gained from the laws of karma and reincarnation. Already there is a tendency in human beings to produce withering bodies, which in the future would become increasingly rickety, even in the very bones. Marrow will be brought to the bones, forces of life to the nerves, by this new revelation, whose value will not reside merely in theories but in its life-giving forces—above all in those of hope.

Faith, love, and hope constitute three stages in the essential being of humankind; they are necessary for health and for life as a whole, for without them we cannot exist. Just as work cannot be done in a dark room until light is obtained, it is equally impossible for human beings to carry on in their fourfold nature if their three sheaths are not permeated, warmed through, and strengthened by faith, love, and hope. For faith, love, and hope are the basic forces in our astral body, our etheric body, and our physical body. And from this one instance you can judge how the new revelation makes its entry into the world, permeating the old language with thought content. Are not these three wonderful words urged upon us in the Gospel revelation, these words of wisdom that ring through the ages—faith, love, hope? But little has been understood of their whole connection with human life, so little that only in certain places has their right sequence been observed.

It is true that faith, love, and hope are sometimes put in this correct order; but the significance of the words is so little appreciated that we often hear faith, hope, love, which is incorrect, for you cannot say astral body, physical body, etheric body, if you would give them their right sequence. That would be putting things higgledy-piggledy, as a child will sometimes do before it understands the thought content of what is said. It is the same with everything relating to the second revelation. It is permeated throughout with thought, and we have striven to permeate with thought our explanation of the Gospels. For what have they meant for people up to now? They have been something with which to fortify humankind and to fill it with great and powerful perceptions, something to inspire human beings to enter the depth of heart and feeling in the Mystery of Golgotha. But now consider the simple fact that people have only just begun to reflect upon the Gospels, and in doing so they have straightway found contradictions, which spiritual science alone can help to illuminate. Thus it is only now that they are beginning to let their souls be worked on by the thought content of what the Gospels give them in a language of the supersensible worlds. In this connection we have pointed out what is so essential and of such consequence for our age: the new appearance of the Christ in an etheric body, for his appearance in a physical body is ruled out by the whole character of our times. Hence we have indicated that the Christ, in contradistinction as it were to the suffering Christ on Golgotha, is appearing now as Christ triumphant, Christ the Lord of Karma. This has been foreshadowed by those who have painted him as the Christ of the Last Judgment. Whether painted or described in words, something is represented that will come to pass at the appointed time.

In truth, this begins in the twentieth century and will hold good until the end of the Earth. It is in our twentieth century that this judgment, this ordering of karma, begins, and we have seen how infinitely important it is for our age that this revelation come to human beings in such a way that even concepts such as faith, love, and hope can be given their true valuation for the first time.

John the Baptist said: "Change your mood of soul for the Kingdom of Heaven is at hand." In other words, accept the human I that no longer needs to avoid approaching the spiritual world. This is a saying that clearly points to what is in question here—that, with the event of Palestine, the time came for the supersensible to pour light into the human I; thus the heavens are able to descend into the I. Previously, the I could come to human beings only by sinking into their unconscious. But those who interpret everything materialistically say that the Christ dealt with the weaknesses, errors, and prejudices of his contemporaries—that he even foretold (like the credulous people of his time) the realization of the millennium or of a great catastrophe for the Earth. Neither of these events, however, occurred; there was indeed a catastrophe, but it was perceptible only to the spirit. The credulous and superstitious, who believe Christ foretold that his actual coming would be from the clouds, interpreted his meaning in a materialistic way,

Today, also, there are people who thus interpret what is to be grasped only in spirit, and when nothing happens in a material sense they judge the matter in just the same way as was done in the case of the millennium. How many indeed we find today who, speaking almost pityingly of those events, say that Christ was influenced by the beliefs of his time and looked for the impending approach to Earth of the Kingdom of Heaven. That was a weakness on Christ's part, they say, and then it was seen—and remarked upon even by distinguished theologians—that the Kingdom of Heaven has not come down on Earth.

It may be that people will meet our new revelation as well in such a way that after a time, when the enhancement of human faculties is in full swing, they will say, "Well, nothing has come of all these predictions of yours," not realizing that they just cannot see what is there. Thus do events repeat themselves. Spiritual science is meant to gather together a large number of people until the fulfillment of what has been said by those with a right knowledge of how the new revelation and new supersensible facts are appearing in human evolution during this century. They will then continue their course in the same way, becoming ever more significant throughout the next three thousand years, until weighty new facts will once more be revealed to humankind.

9.

FAITH, LOVE, HOPE

II

DECEMBER 3, 1911, NUREMBERG

from *Faith, Love, Hope*

YESTERDAY we tried to assess the importance in human life of what may be called the "supersensible revelation" of our time. We suggested that this revelation was to be considered the third in the most recent cycle of humanity, and that it should, in a certain sense, be regarded as sequential to the Sinai revelation and the revelation at the time of the Mystery of Golgotha. We should not think that this aspect of our age merely has theoretical or scientific effect on us. As anthroposophists, we must rise to an ever fuller realization that human beings are neglecting something essential in their evolution by remaining aloof from everything announced to us now and in the future.

It is certainly befitting that the external world should initially pass this by, and even treat it as pure fantasy; and it is quite natural as well that many people would at first ignore the harmful consequences of disregarding what is here in question. Anthroposophists, however, should be clear that the souls now dwelling in human bodies, regardless of what they absorb at present, are approaching a certain future. What I have to say concerns every soul, for it is part of the whole trend of change in our time. Souls incarnated today have only recently advanced to the stage of genuine I-consciousness; this has been in preparation during the course of evolution since the old Atlantean period. From those ancient days until the time of the great change intimated by the Mystery of Golgotha, this I-consciousness was gradually liberating itself from a consciousness no longer really known by contemporary human beings. Today people typically distinguish only between the ordinary state of wakefulness and that of sleep, when consciousness is completely suspended. Between these conditions, people also recognize the intermediate state of dreaming. From a modern perspective, however, this is regarded only as a kind of aberration, or departure from the norm. Through dream images, certain events from the depths of the soul life rise into consciousness; but in ordinary dreaming they emerge in such an obscure form that the dreamer is seldom able to interpret correctly their very real relationship to deep, supersensible processes in the soul's life.

In order to grasp one characteristic feature of this intermediate state—a state well understood in earlier times—let us take an ordinary dream, which has been made a regular riddle by modern scientific investigators of dreams, who can only interpret it superficially and materialistically. A highly significant dream; you see, I am taking my example from the science of dreams, which, as I mentioned before, today has been given a place (little understood though it is) among sciences such as chemistry and physics. The following dream, one that is characteristic, has been recorded. I might easily have taken my example from similar unpublished dreams, but I want to deal with one that raises certain problems for modern commentators with no key to such matters.

The case is this: a married couple had a much beloved son and were enjoying his growth. One day he became ill, and his condition grew worse within a few hours to the degree that, by the end of that day, he passed through the gate of death. Consequently, the couple's ordinary experience was that their son was snatched from them abruptly, torn from a life full of promise. Of course, the parents mourned for their son. During the following months both parents had quite a few dreams that reminded them of him. But one night after quite a long time, many, many months after his death, the boy's father and mother had exactly the same dream. They dreamed that their son had appeared to them and told them he had been buried alive, having only been in a trance, and that they merely had to look into the matter to be convinced that this was true. The parents told each other what they had dreamed on the same night, and their attitude to life was such that they immediately asked the authorities for permission to have their son's body disinterred. The request was refused, however, which gave the parents even more cause for grief.

The investigator who gave his account of the dream could think of it only in a materialistic way, and he was faced with great difficulties. His final explanation is quite remarkable and bound to seem contrived to anyone who reads it. He said: We have to assume that one parent had the dream, and the other, hearing it while awake, got the idea that he or she had dreamed it as well. To contemporary consciousness, this interpretation initially seems fairly obvious, but it doesn't go very deep. I have specifically mentioned that, for anyone well versed in dream experiences, it is not unusual for several people to have the same dream at the same time.

Let us try now to look into this dream experience from the perspective of spiritual science. The results of spiritual investigation show how one who has gone through the gate of death lives on as an individual in the spiritual world. We also know that there are definite connections between every thing and every being in the world, and that this is shown by the link that unites those who have departed with people still on Earth who lovingly concentrate thoughts on their dead. There is no doubt that there is a connection between those on the physical plane and those who have left it for the supersensible world. There is always a connection whenever those left on the physical plane turn their thoughts to the dead—a connection that may continue even when their thoughts are directed elsewhere.

The point is this: human beings, as they are organized for life on the physical plane, cannot become conscious of these bonds while awake. Lacking knowledge of a thing, however, does not justify a denial of its existence; such a conclusion would be very superficial. On that basis, those now sitting in this room and not seeing Nuremberg could easily prove there is no such place. So we must be clear that it is only because of their present-day organization that human beings know nothing of their connection with the dead; nevertheless, it exists.

However, knowledge of what is going on in the depths of the soul can occasionally be conjured up into consciousness, and this happens in dreams. It is one thing we have to reckon with when considering dream experiences. Another thing is the knowledge that passing through death is not the sudden leap imagined by those who know nothing about it; it is a gradual transition. What occupies a soul here on Earth does not then vanish in a moment. What a person loves, he or she continues to love after death. But there is then no possibility of satisfying a feeling that depends for its satisfaction on a physical body. The wishes and desires of the soul, its joys and sorrows, the particular tendencies it has during incarnation in a physical body—these naturally continue even when the gate of death has been passed. We can therefore understand the strength of the feeling in this young man, meeting with death when quite unprepared, that he would like to be still on Earth, and how keen was his longing to be in a physical body. This desire, working as a force in the soul, lasted for a long, long time during his kamaloka.

Now picture vividly to yourselves the parents, with their thoughts engrossed by this beloved dead son. Even in sleep the connecting links were there. Just at the moment when both father and mother began to dream, the son, in accordance with the state of his soul, had a particularly keen desire that we may perhaps clothe in these words: "Oh! If only I were still on Earth in a physical body." This thought from the dead son sank deep into his parents' souls, but they had no special faculty for understanding what lay behind the dream. Thus the imprint of the thought on their soul life was transformed into familiar images. If they could have clearly perceived what the son was pouring into their souls, their interpretation would have been: "Our son is longing just now for a physical body." In fact, the dream image clothed itself in words they could understand—"He has been buried alive!"—which hid the truth from them.

Thus, in dream pictures of this kind we should not look for an exact replica of what is real in the spiritual worlds; we must expect the actual objective occurrence to be veiled according to the dreamer's degree of understanding. Today it is the peculiar feature of the dreamworld that, if we are unable to go into these matters more deeply, we can no longer regard its pictures as faithful copies of what underlies them. We are obliged to say that something is always living in our soul behind the dream picture, and that the picture can be looked upon only as an even greater illusion than the external world confronting us when we are awake.

It is only in our time that dreams are appearing to people in this guise—strictly speaking, only since the events in Palestine, when I-consciousness took on the form it has now. Before then, the pictures appeared while people were in a state different from either waking or sleeping, a third state, more like the one prevailing in the supersensible world. Human beings lived with the dead in spirit far more than is feasible now. There is no need to look back many centuries before the Christian era to realize what a countless number of people were then able to say: "The dead are certainly not dead; they are living in the supersensible world. I can perceive what they are feeling and seeing, what they now actually are. This holds good also for the other beings in the supersensible world, for instance, those we know as the Hierarchies."

Thus, human beings once had these experiences, in certain states between waking and sleeping, and the last degenerate echoes linger on in dreams. It was very important that humans should feel this disappearance of something they once possessed. In the traditional epoch of human evolution when the great events were taking place in Palestine, there was indeed cause for saying, "Change your mood of soul; quite different times are coming for humankind." And among the changes was this—that the old possibility of seeing into the spiritual world, of personally experiencing how matters stood with the dead and with all other spiritual beings, was going to pass away.

The history of those bygone days offers ample evidence of this living with the dead—notably in the religious veneration that arose everywhere in the form of ancestor worship. This was founded on belief in the reality and activity of those who had died, which continued almost everywhere during the transitional period. Human experience was this, though perhaps not put clearly into words: Formerly our souls could rise to the world we call the spirit world, and we were able to dwell among the higher beings and with the dead. But now our dead leave us in quite another sense; they disappear from our consciousness and the old vivid contact is no more.

We come here to something exceptionally difficult to grasp, but the intelligent mind, the intelligent soul, can learn to do so. Those who felt most vividly the loss of direct psychic contact with the dead were the early Christians, and this was what made their worship of God so full of meaning, so infinitely deep and holy. They compensated for what was lost by the reverent feeling they brought to their religious ceremonies, for instance, when they sacrified at the graves of their dead or celebrated the Mass or observed any other religious rite. In fact, it was during this period of transition, when consciousness of the dead was seen to be wanting, that altars took the shape of coffins. Thus it was with this kind of feeling for mortal remains—unlike that of the ancient Egyptians—that the service of God, the service of the spirit, was reverently performed. As I have said, this is something not easy to understand. However, we need only observe the form of an altar and allow our hearts to respond to this gradual change in the whole outlook of humanity, and then feeling and understanding will arise for the change and its consequences.

We see, therefore, that slowly, gradually, the present state of the human soul was brought about. From indications given yesterday it can be gathered that what has thus come into being will again be succeeded by a different state, for which people are already developing faculties. The example I gave yesterday of how people will see, in a kind of dream picture, their future karmic compensation for some deed, means the reawakening of faculties that will lead the soul once more to the spiritual worlds. In relation to earthly evolution as a whole, the intermediate state when the soul has been cut off from the supersensible world will prove to be comparatively short. It had to come about for human beings to be able to acquire the strongest possible forces for their freedom. But something else I have spoken of was bound up with the whole progress of human evolution—only in this way were human beings able to acquire a feeling of the I within them, to have the right I-consciousness. The farther human beings advance into the future, the more firmly will this I-consciousness establish itself within them, always increasing in significance. In other words, the force and self-sufficiency of human individuality will be increasingly accentuated, so that it becomes necessary for human beings to find in themselves their own effective support. Thus we see that the I-consciousness human beings have today does not go back as far as is usually imagined. Only a few incarnations ago, humans did not have the I-feeling that is characteristic of them today. And since the I-feeling is intimately connected with memory, we need not be surprised that many people have not yet begun to look back on their previous incarnations. Because of the undeveloped state of this feeling for the I during early childhood, people do not even remember what happened to them then, so it seems quite comprehensible that, for the same reasons, they are unable yet to remember their earlier incarnations. But now we have come to the point when human beings have developed a feeling for their I, and the forces are unfolding that will make it necessary in our coming incarnations to remember those that have gone before. The days are drawing near when people will feel bound to admit: We have strange glimpses into the past, when we were already on the Earth but living in another bodily form; we look back and have to say that we were already then on Earth. And among the faculties appearing more and more in human beings will be one that arouses the feeling: It can only be that I am looking back on my earlier incarnations.

Just think how in the human souls now on Earth the inner force is already arising that will enable them to look back in their next incarnations and recognize themselves. But for those who have not become familiar with the idea of reincarnation, this looking back will be a veritable torment. Ignorance of the mysteries of repeated earthly lives will be actually painful for these human beings; forces in them are striving to rise and bear witness to earlier times, but this cannot happen because all knowledge of those forces is refused. Not to learn of the truths now being proclaimed through spiritual science does not mean neglecting mere theories; it is on the way to making a torment of life in future incarnations. Accordingly, something is happening in these times of transition; the slow preparation for it can be gathered from our second mystery play, *The Soul's Probation*, where earlier incarnations of the characters are portrayed, incarnations of only a few centuries before. The event was then already in preparation; and now, thanks to the wisdom of cosmic guidance, human beings will be given positive opportunities to make themselves familiar with the truths of the Mysteries.

At present, comparatively few find their way to spiritual science; their number is modest compared with the rest of humankind. It may be said that interest in anthroposophy is not yet very widespread. But, in our age, the law of reincarnation is such that those now going through the world apathetically, ignoring what experience can tell about the need for exploring the riddles of life, will incarnate again in a relatively short time, and thus have ample opportunity for absorbing the truths of spiritual science. That is how it stands. So when perhaps we see around us people we esteem, people we love, who will have nothing to do with anthroposophy, are even hostile toward it, we ought not to take it too much to heart. It is perfectly true, and should be realized by anthroposophists, that refusing to look into spiritual science, or anthroposophy, means preparing a life of torment for future incarnations on Earth. That is true, and should not be treated lightly. On the other hand, those who see friends and acquaintances they care for showing no inclination toward anthroposophy can think, "If I become a good anthroposophist myself, I will find an early opportunity, with the forces remaining to me after death, to prove helpful to these souls"—provided the living link we have spoken of is there. And because the interval between death and rebirth is becoming shorter, these souls too will have the opportunity of absorbing the Mystery truths that must be absorbed if torment is to be avoided in future human incarnations. All is not yet lost. Therefore, we have to look upon anthroposophy as a real power, yet on the other hand we must not be unduly grieved or pessimistic about the matter.

It would be mistaken optimism to say, "If that is how things are, I need not accept the truths of spiritual science till my next incarnation." If everyone were to say that, there would be too few opportunities for effective aid to be given when the next incarnations gradually come. Even if those wishing for anthroposophy can now receive its truths from only a very few people, the situation will be different for the countless hosts who, in a comparatively short time, will be eagerly turning to it. A countless number of anthroposophists will then be needed to make these truths known, either here on the physical plane or—if they are not incarnated—from higher planes. That is one thing we must learn from the whole character of the great change now taking place. The other is that all this has to be experienced by the I so that it will rely increasingly upon itself, becoming more and more independent. The self-reliance of the I must come for all souls; but it will mean disaster for those who make no effort to learn about the great spiritual truths, for they will feel the increasing individualism as isolation. On the other hand, those who have made themselves familiar with the deep mysteries of the spiritual world will thereby find a way to forge ever stronger spiritual bonds between souls. Old bonds will be loosened, new ones formed. All this is imminent, but it will be gradual.

We are living at present in the fifth post-Atlantean period, which will be followed by a sixth and then by a seventh, when a catastrophe will come upon us, just as one came between the Atlantean and post-Atlantean periods. When the lectures on the Apocalypse were given here in Nuremberg, you heard a description of this coming catastrophe, of how it will resemble and how it will differ from the one in old Atlantis.

If we observe life around us, we might express the particular feature of our age in this way: The most active element in human beings today is their intellectualism, their intellectual conception of the world. We are living altogether in an age of intellectualism. It has been brought about through quite special circumstances, and we will come to understand these if we look back to the time before our present fifth post-Atlantean cultural epoch, the Greco-Latin, as it is called. That was the remarkable period when human beings had not reached their present state of detachment from the manifestations of nature and knowledge of the world. But at the same time it was the epoch when the I descended among humankind. The Christ event had also to happen in that epoch, because, with Him, the I made its descent in a special way.

What then is our present experience? It is not just of the entry of the I; we now experience how one of our sheaths casts a kind of reflection upon the soul. The sheath that yesterday we called the "faith body" throws its reflection onto the human soul in this fifth epoch. Thus, it is a feature of present-day humanity that we have something in the soul that is, as it were, a reflection of the faith nature of the astral body. In the sixth post-Atlantean epoch there will be a reflection within human beings of the love nature of the etheric body, and in the seventh, before the great catastrophe, the reflection of the hope nature of the physical body.

For those who have heard lectures I am now giving in various places, I would note that these gradual happenings have been described from a different perspective, both in Munich and in Stuttgart.[1] The theme, however, is always the same. What is now being portrayed in connection with the three great human forces, Faith, Love, and Hope, was there represented in direct relation to the elements in a human life of soul; but it is all the same thing. I have done this intentionally, so that anthroposophists may grow accustomed to getting the gist of a matter without strict adherence to special words. When we realize that things can be described from many different sides, we will no longer pin so much faith on words and will focus our efforts on the matter itself, knowing that any description amounts to only an approximation of the whole truth. Adherence to the original

---

1. Steiner was currently presenting the course of lectures *Esoteric Christianity and the Mission of Christian Rosenkreutz* (Rudolf Steiner Press, London, 1984).

words is the last thing that can help us get to the heart of a matter. The one helpful means is to harmonize what has been said in successive lectures, just as we learn about a tree by studying it not from one direction only but from many different aspects. Thus the essential characteristic of our time is the force of faith of the astral body that is shining into the soul. Someone might say: "That is rather strange. You are telling us now that the ruling force of the age is faith. We might admit this is the case for those who hold to old beliefs, but today so many people are too mature for that, and they look down on such old beliefs as belonging to the childish stage of human evolution." It may well be that people who say they are monists believe they do not believe, but actually they are more ready to believe than those calling themselves believers. For, though monists are not conscious of it, all that we see in the various forms of monism is belief of the most blind kind, which monists believe to be knowledge. We cannot describe their doings at all without mentioning belief. And, quite apart from the belief of those who believe they do not believe, we find that, strictly speaking, an endless amount of what is most important today is connected with the reflection the astral body throws into the soul, giving it the character of ardent faith. We have only to call to mind lives of the great people of our age. For example, Richard Wagner, even as an artist, was rising all his life to a definite faith; it is fascinating to watch this in the development of his personality. Everywhere we look today, the lights and shadows can be interpreted as the reflection of faith in what we may call the human I-soul.

Our age will be followed by one in which the need for love will cast its light. Love in the sixth cultural epoch will show itself in a very different form—different even from what can be called Christian love. Slowly we draw nearer to that epoch; and by making those in the anthroposophical movement familiar with the mysteries of the cosmos, with the nature of the various individualities both on the physical plane and on the higher planes, we try to kindle love for everything in existence. This is not done so much by talking of love, as by feeling that what is able to kindle love in the soul is prepared for the sixth epoch by anthroposophy. Through anthroposophy, the forces of love are especially aroused in the whole human soul, and what a person needs is prepared for by gradually acquiring a true understanding of the Mystery of Golgotha. For it is indeed true that the Mystery of Golgotha came to pass; and the Gospels have evoked something that yesterday was likened to how children learn to speak. But the deepest lesson—the mission of earthly love in its connection with the Mystery of Golgotha—has not yet been grasped. Full understanding of this will be possible only in the sixth post-Atlantean cultural epoch, when people grow to realize more and more that its foundations are actually within them, and out of their innermost being—in other words, out of love—do what should be done. Then the guidance of the Ten Commandments will have been outlived and the stage reached that is described in Goethe's words: "Duty—when one loves the commands one gives to oneself." When forces wake in our souls that impel us to do what we should through love alone, we discover in us something that must gradually become widespread in the sixth cultural epoch. Then special forces of the etheric body will make themselves known in a person's nature.

To understand what it is that must increasingly come about in this way, we have to consider it from two sides, One side has certainly not come yet and is only dreamt of by the most advanced in spirit; it is a well-defined relation between custom, morals, ethics, and the understanding, intellectuality. Today a person may be to a certain extent a rascal, yet at the same time intelligent and clever. Some people may even use their very cleverness to further their knavery. At present people are not required to combine their intelligence with an equal degree of morality. To all we have been anticipating for the future it must be added that as we advance it will no longer be possible for these two qualities of the human soul to be kept apart, or to exist in unequal measure. Those who, according to the reckoning of their previous incarnation, have become particularly intelligent without being moral will in their new incarnation possess only a stunted intelligence. To have equal amounts of intelligence and morality in future incarnations they will be obliged, as a consequence of universal cosmic law, to enter their new incarnation with a crippled intelligence, so that immorality and stupidity coincide. For immorality has a crippling effect upon intelligence. In other words, we are approaching the age when morality and what has now been described for the sixth post-Atlantean epoch as the shining into the I-soul of the love forces of the etheric body, point essentially to forces having to do with harmonizing those of intelligence and morality. That is the one side to be considered.

The other side is that it is solely through harmony of this kind, between morality, custom, and intelligence, that the whole depth of the Mystery of Golgotha is to be grasped. This will come about only through the individuality who, before Christ Jesus came to Earth, prepared human beings for that Mystery, developing in his successive incarnations ever greater powers as teacher of the greatest of all earthly events. This individuality, whom in his rank as Bodhisattva we call the successor of Gautama Buddha, was incarnated in the personality living about a hundred years before Christ under the name of Jeshu ben Pandira. Among his many students was one who had at that time already, in a certain sense, written down a prophetic version of the Matthew Gospel, and this, after the Mystery of Golgotha had been enacted, needed only to be given a new form.

There have been and will continue to be frequent incarnations of the individuality who appeared as Jeshu ben Pandira, until he rises from the rank of Bodhisattva to that of Buddha. According to our reckoning of time, this will be in about three thousand years; then a sufficient number of people will possess the above-mentioned faculties, and, in the course of a remarkable incarnation, this great teacher of humankind will be able to interpret the Mystery of Golgotha in a very different way from what is possible today. It is true that even today a seer into the supersensible worlds can gain some idea of what is to happen then; but the ordinary earthly organization of the human being cannot yet provide a physical body capable of doing what that teacher will be able to do approximately three thousand years hence. There is as yet no human language through which verbal teaching could exert the magical effects that will spring from the words of that great teacher of humanity. His words will flow directly to the hearts of human beings, into their souls, like a healing medicine; nothing in those words will be merely theoretical. At the same time the teaching will contain, to an extent far greater than can be conceived today, a magical moral force carrying to hearts and souls a full conviction of the eternal, deeply significant communion of intellect and morality.

This great teacher, who will be able to give to human beings ripe for it the most profound instruction concerning the nature of the Mystery of Golgotha, will fulfil what Oriental prophets have always said—that the true successor of Buddha would be, for all humankind, the greatest teacher of the good. For that reason he has been called in Oriental tradition the Maitreya Buddha. His task will be to enlighten human beings concerning the Mystery of Golgotha, and for this he will draw ideas and words of the deepest significance from the very language he will use. No human language today can evoke any conception of it. His words will imprint into human souls directly, magically, the nature of the Mystery of Golgotha. In this connection also we are approaching what we may call the future moral age of humankind; in a certain sense we could designate it as a coming Golden Age.

Even today, however, speaking from the ground of athroposophy, we point in full consciousness to what is destined to come about—how the Christ will gradually reveal himself to ever higher powers in human beings, and how the teachers, who up to now have taught only individual peoples and individual human beings, will become the interpreters of the great Christ event for all who are willing to listen. And we can point out how, through the dawning of the age of love, conditions for the age of morality are prepared.

Then will come the last epoch, during which human souls will receive the reflection of what we call hope—when, strengthened through the force flowing from the Mystery of Golgotha and from the age of morality, human beings will take into themselves forces of hope. This is the most important gift they need in order to face the next catastrophe and to begin new life, just as was done in this present post-Atlantean age. When in the final post-Atlantean epoch our external culture, with its tendency to calculation, will have come to a climax that brings no feeling of satisfaction but leaves those who have not developed the spiritual within them to confront their culture in utter desolation—then out of spirituality the seed of hope will be sown, and in the next period of human evolution it will grow to maturity. If the spirit is denied all possibility of imparting to human souls what it can give, and what the anthroposophical movement has the will to convey, this external culture might for a short while be able to hold its own. Ultimately, however, people will ask themselves what they have gained and say: "We have wireless installations, undreamed of by our ancestors, to transmit our thoughts all over the Earth, and what good does it do us? The most trivial, unproductive thoughts are sent hither and thither, and human ingenuity has to be strained to the utmost to enable us to travel at high speeds around the globe or to transport something for us to eat from some far distant region, using all kinds of perfected appliances. But there is nothing in our heads worth sending from place to place, for our thoughts are cheerless; moreover, since we have had our present means of communication, they have become even more cheerless than when they were conveyed in the old snail-like fashion."

In short, despair and desolation are all that our civilization can spread over the Earth. But, in the last cultural epoch, souls who have accepted the spiritual in life will have become enriched, as if on the ruins of the external life of culture. Their surety that this acceptance of the spiritual has not been in vain will be the strong force of hope within them—hope that after a great catastrophe a new age will come for human beings, when there will appear in external life, in a new culture, what has already been prepared spiritually within the soul.

Thus, if we permeate our whole being with spiritual science, we will advance step by step, in full consciousness, from our age of faith, through the age of love and the age of hope, to what we can see approaching us as the highest, truest, most beautiful goals of humanity.

* * *

Freedom and Love

Extract of a lecture

NUREMBERG, JUNE 30, 1908

from *The Apocalypse of St. John*

...If it were impossible for humans to sink into the abyss of evil, then what on the one hand we call love and on the other freedom would also be unattainable for them. To the esotericist, freedom is inseparably connected with the concept of love. Love would be impossible for human beings and freedom would be impossible for them without the possibility of sailing down into the abyss. A person unable to freely choose good or evil would be only a being led on a leash to a good that must be attained due to necessity, a being with no power to choose the good from a fully purified will, through the love that springs from freedom. If it were impossible for human beings to follow the trail of the monster with the two horns, it would also be impossible for them to follow God out of their own individual love. It was in accordance with a wise Providence that the possibility of freedom was given to a humankind that has been developing through our planetary system, and this possibility of freedom could be given on no other condition than that human beings themselves have to make the free choice between good and evil.

But this is only an empty theory, you might say, and humans rise only slowly to the point where they not only say this in words and accept it in moments of speculation as a kind of explanation, but also experience it in their feeling. Seldom do people now rise to the thought, *I thank you, O wise Providence, that you have made it possible for me to bring you a love that is not forced but springs up free in my own breast; that you do not force me to love you, but have given me the choice of following you.*

10.
Love and Its Meaning in the World

DECEMBER 17, 1912, ZÜRICH

When we say that, at this point in human evolution, people must come to understand the Christ impulse, we may ask: What, then, is the situation for those who have never heard of the Christ impulse and may have never even heard the name of Christ? Will such people be deprived of the Christ impulse because they have not heard the name of Christ? Is it necessary to have some theoretical knowledge of the Christ impulse for Christ's power to flow into the soul? We will become clear about these questions by the following thoughts concerning human life from birth until death.

Human beings come into the world and live through early childhood half asleep. Gradually, they must learn to experience themselves as I—to find their bearings as I-beings and enrich their soul life constantly by what is received through the I. By the time death approaches, this soul life is richest and ripest. Hence, the vital question: What about our soul life after the body falls away? It is peculiar to our physical and soul life that the wealth of our experience and knowledge increases in significance the nearer we approach death; but at the same time certain attributes are lost and replaced by others of an entirely different character.

During our youth we gather knowledge, pass through experiences, cherish hopes that, as a rule, can only later be fulfilled. As we grow older, we begin more and more to love the wisdom revealed by life. Love of wisdom is not egoistic, for this love increases as we approach death. As our expectation of gaining something through wisdom decreases, wisdom increases—our love for this content of soul steadily increases. In this sense, spiritual science may in fact become a source of temptation to the degree that a person may come to believe that the next life will depend on acquiring wisdom in the present one. The effect of spiritual science may be an extension of egoism beyond the bounds of the present life, and this is the danger. Consequently, when understood in the wrong way, spiritual science may become a tempter; this is there in its very nature.

Love of wisdom acquired from life may be compared to the flowering of a plant at the proper stage of maturity. Love arises for something within ourselves. Human beings have often tried to sublimate the impulse of love for something within themselves. We find evidence, for example, of mystics who attempted to transform the urge toward self-love into the love of wisdom, and to let this love shine out in beauty. By sinking through contemplation into the depths of their own soul life, they worked for awareness of the divine spark within themselves. The truth, however, is that the wisdom one acquires in life is merely the means to unfold the seed of the next life. When a plant has completed its growth through the year, the seed remains, and this is also true of the wisdom acquired from life. A human being passes through the gate of death, and the ripening process of the spiritual core of its being is the seed of the next life. Those who feel this may become mystics and mistake what is only the seed of the next life for the divine spark, or Absolute. This is their interpretation, because it goes against the grain for human beings to acknowledge that this spirit seed is simply their own self. Because they knew nothing of reincarnation, Meister Eckhart, John Tauler, and others spoke of it as the "God within." When we understand the significance of the law of reincarnation, we recognize the purpose of love in the world, both in a particular and in a general sense. When we speak of karma, we mean the cause in the one life that affects the next. Neverthless, we cannot truly speak of love in terms of "cause and effect." We cannot speak of an act of love and its eventual compensation. True, if there is an action, there will be compensation, but this has nothing to do with love itself. Acts of love do not look for compensation in the next life.

Imagine, for example, that we work, and this leads to gain. It may also happen that our work gives us no joy, since we do it merely to pay our debts, not for actual reward. We can imagine that in this way we have already spent what we are now earning through our work. We would prefer to have no debts, but as things stand, we are obliged to work in order to pay them. Now let us apply this example to our actions in general. By everything we do out of love we pay off debts. From an esoteric point of view, what is done out of love brings no reward but makes amends for profit already expended. The only actions from which we have nothing in the future are those we perform out of true, genuine love. This truth may well be disquieting and human beings are lucky in that they know nothing of it in their upper consciousness. But in their subconsciousness all of them know it, and that is why acts of love are done so unwillingly, why there is so little love in the world. Human beings feel instinctively that they may expect nothing for their I in the future from acts of love. An advanced stage of development must be reached before the soul can experience joy in performing acts of love from which there is nothing to be gained for itself. The impulse for this is not strong in humankind. But esotericism can be a source of powerful incentives for acts of love.

Our egoism gains nothing from acts of love, but the world gains all the more. Esotericism tells us that love is to the world what the Sun is for outer life. No soul could thrive if love departed from the world. Love is the "moral" Sun of the world. Would it not be absurd if a person who delights in the flowers growing in a meadow were to wish that the Sun would vanish from the world? Translated into terms of the moral life, this means that our deep concern must be that an impulse for sound, healthy development shall find its way into human affairs. To disseminate love over the Earth in the greatest measure possible, to promote love on the Earth—that and that alone is wisdom.

What do we learn from spiritual science? We learn about the evolution of the Earth, we hear of the Spirit of the Earth, the Earth's surface and its changing conditions, the development of the human body, and so on. We come to understand the nature of the forces working and weaving in the evolutionary process. What does this mean? What does it mean when people do not want to know anything about spiritual science? It means that they have no interest in reality. For one can know nothing about the Earth if there is no desire to know anything about the nature of Old Saturn, Old Sun, and Old Moon. Lack of interest in the world is egoism in its grossest form. Interest in all existence is humanity's duty. Let us therefore long for and love the Sun with its creative power, its love for the well-being of the Earth and the souls of human beings. This interest in the Earth's evolution should be the spiritual seed of love for the world. A spiritual science without love would be a danger to humankind. But love should not be a matter for preaching; love must and indeed will come into the world through the spreading of knowledge of spiritual truths. Acts of love and spiritual science should be inseparably united.

Love mediated by the senses is the wellspring of creative power, of what is coming into being. Without sense-born love, nothing material would exist in the world; without spiritual love, nothing spiritual can arise in evolution. When we practice love, cultivate love, creative forces pour into the world. Can the intellect be expected to offer reasons for this? The creative forces poured into the world before we ourselves and our intellect came into being. True, as egoists, we can deprive the future of creative forces; but we cannot obliterate the acts of love and the creative forces of the past. We owe our existence to acts of love done in the past. The strength with which we have been endowed by these acts of love is the measure of our deep debt to the past, and whatever love we may at any time be able to bring forth is payment of debts owed for our existence. In the light of this knowledge we will be able to understand the actions of those who have reached a high stage of development, for they have still greater debts to pay to the past. They pay their debts through acts of love, and herein lies their wisdom. The higher the stage of development reached by human beings, the more the impulse of love in them increases in strength; wisdom alone does not suffice.

Let us think of the meaning and effect of love in the world in the following way. Love is always a reminder of debts owed to life in the past, and because we gain nothing for the future by paying off these debts, no profit for ourselves accrues from our acts of love. We have to leave our acts of love behind in the world; but they are then a spiritual factor in the flow of world events. It is not through our acts of love but through acts of a different character that we perfect ourselves; yet the world is richer for our acts of love. *Love is the creative force in the world.*

Besides love there are two other powers in the world. How do they compare with love? One is strength, might; the other is wisdom. In regard to strength or might we can speak of degrees: weaker, stronger, or absolute might—omnipotence. The same applies to wisdom, for there are stages on the path to omniscience. It will not do to speak in the same way of degrees of love. What is universal love, love for all beings? In the case of love we cannot speak of enhancement as we can speak of enhancement of knowledge into omniscience or of might into omnipotence, by virtue of which we attain greater perfection of our own being. Love for a few or for many beings has nothing to do with our own perfecting. Love for everything that lives cannot be compared with omnipotence; the concept of magnitude, or of enhancement, cannot rightly be applied to love. Can the attribute of omnipotence be ascribed to the Divine Being who lives and weaves through the world? Contentions born of feeling must here be silent: were God omnipotent, he would be responsible for everything that happens and there could be no human freedom. If human beings can be free, then certainly there can be no divine omnipotence.

Is the Godhead omniscient? Since our highest goal is likeness to God, our striving must be in the direction of omniscience. Is omniscience, then, the supreme treasure? If it is, a vast chasm must forever yawn between human beings and God. If the Godhead possessed the supreme treasure of omniscience for itself and withheld it from us, we would have to be aware of that chasm at every moment. The all-encompassing attribute of the

Godhead is not omnipotence, nor is it omniscience—it is *love,* the attribute that cannot be enhanced. God is uttermost love, unalloyed love, is born as it were out of love, is the very substance and essence of love. God is pure love, not supreme wisdom, not supreme might. God has retained love for himself but has shared wisdom and might with Lucifer and Ahriman. He has shared wisdom with Lucifer and might with Ahriman so that human beings may become free, so that under the influence of wisdom they may make progress.

If we try to find the source of anything creative, we arrive at love; love is the ground, the foundation, of everything alive. It is a different impulse in evolution that leads beings to greater widsom and power. We make progress through wisdom and strength. When we study the course of human evolution, we see how the development of wisdom and strength is subject to change—there is evolutionary progress, and then the Christ impulse poured once into humankind through the Mystery of Golgotha. Love did not come into the world by degrees; it flowed into humanity as a gift of the Godhead, completely and perfectly whole. Nevertheless, we can receive that impulse into ourselves gradually. The divine impulse of love as we need it in earthly life is an impulse that came once and forever.

True love is incapable of reduction or amplification. It is very different from wisdom and power. Love does not awaken expectations of the future; it *is* payment of past debts. Such was the Mystery of Golgotha in world evolution. Did the Godhead, then, owe any debt to humanity?

Lucifer's influence introduced a certain element into human beings; the result was to remove something we had possessed previously. This new element led to a descent; the Mystery of Golgotha countered that and made possible the payment of all debts. The impulse of Golgotha was not intended to remove the sins we have committed in evolution, but to counterbalance what crept into humanity through Lucifer.

Imagine that there are people who know nothing of the name of Jesus Christ, nothing of what is communicated in the Gospels, but who understand the radical difference between the nature of wisdom and might and the nature of love. Such people, even though they know nothing of the Mystery of Golgotha, are Christians in the truest sense. A person who knows that love is there to pay debts and brings no profit for the future, is a true Christian. To understand the nature of love—that is to be a Christian. Theosophy, or spiritual science, alone, with its teachings of karma and reincarnation, can make us into great egoists unless the impulse of love, the Christ impulse, is added; only in this way can we acquire the power to overcome the egoism that may be generated by spiritual science. The balance is established by an understanding of the Christ impulse. Spiritual science is given to the world today because it is a necessity for humankind, but it contains the great danger that, if it is cultivated without the Christ impulse, without the impulse of love, human beings will only increase their egoism, will actually breed egoism that lasts even beyond death. We must not conclude from this that we should not cultivate spiritual science; rather we must learn to realize that understanding of the essential nature of love is an integral part of it.

What occurred with the Mystery of Golgotha? Jesus of Nazareth was born, lived as related in the Gospels, and when he was thirty years old he was baptized in the Jordan. Thereafter, the Christ lived for three years in the body of Jesus of Nazareth and fulfilled the Mystery of Golgotha. Many believe that the Mystery of Golgotha should be considered entirely from the human aspect, since they view it as an earthly act, belonging to the realm of Earth. But that is not true. Only from the vantage point of the higher worlds is it possible to see the Mystery of Golgotha in its true light and how it came to pass on the Earth.

Let us think again of the beginning of the evolution of the Earth and humankind. Human beings were endowed with certain spiritual powers, and then Lucifer approached them. We can say that at this point the gods who further the progress of evolution surrendered their omnipotence to Lucifer so that humankind might become free. But human beings sank into matter more deeply than was intended; they slipped away from the gods of progress, fell more deeply than had been wished. How, then, can the gods of progress draw humankind to themselves again? To understand this we must not think of Earth, but of gods taking counsel together. It is for the gods that Christ performs the act through which human beings are drawn back to the gods. Lucifer's deed was enacted in the supersensible world; Christ's deed was enacted in the supersensible world *and* in the physical world. This achievement is beyond the power of any human being. Lucifer's act belongs to the supersensible world. But Christ came down to the Earth to perform his act here, and people are the observers at that deed. The Mystery of Golgotha is an action of the gods, a concern of the gods at which humans are the onlookers. The door of heaven opens and an act of the gods shines through. This is the one and only deed on Earth that is entirely supersensible. No wonder, therefore, that those who do not believe in the supersensible have no belief in Christ's deed. The act of Christ is a deed of the gods, an act that they themselves enact. Herein lies the glory and the unique significance of the Mystery of Golgotha, and human beings are invited to be its witnesses. Historical evidence is not to be found. Humans have seen the event in its external aspect only; but the Gospels were written from vision of the supersensible and are therefore easily disavowed by those who have no feeling for supersensible reality.

The Mystery of Golgotha as an accomplished fact is one of the most sublime of all experiences in the spiritual world. Lucifer's deed belongs to a time when human beings were still aware of their own participation in the supersensible world; Christ's deed was performed in material existence itself—it is both a physical and a spiritual action. We can understand the deed of Lucifer through wisdom; understanding of the Mystery of Golgotha is beyond the reach of wisdom alone. Even if all the wisdom of this world is ours, the deed of Christ may still be beyond our comprehension. *Love* is essential for any understanding of the Mystery of Golgotha. Only when love streams into wisdom and then again wisdom flows into love will it be possible to grasp the nature and meaning of the Mystery of Golgotha—only when, as they live on toward death, human beings unfold love of wisdom. Love united with wisdom—that is what we need when we pass through the gate of death, because without wisdom that is united with love we die in very truth. *Philo-sophia,* philosophy, is love of wisdom. The ancient wisdom was not philosophy for it was not born through love but through revelation. There is no such thing as philosophy of the East—but wisdom of the East, yes. Philosophy as love of wisdom came into the world with Christ; there we have the entry of wisdom emanating from the impulse of love that came into the world as the Christ impulse. The impulse of love must now be carried into effect in wisdom itself.

The ancient wisdom, acquired by the seer through revelation, is expressed in the sublime words from the original prayer of humankind: *Ex Deo Nascimur,* Out of God we are born. That is ancient wisdom. Christ, who came forth from the realms of spirit, has united wisdom with love, and this love will overcome egoism. Such is its aim. But it must be offered independently and freely from one being to the other. Hence the beginning of the era of love coincided with the beginning of the era of egoism. The cosmos has its source and origin in love; egoism was the natural and inevitable offshoot of love. Yet with time the Christ impulse, the impulse of love, will overcome the element of separation that has crept into the world, and the human being can gradually become a participant in this force of love. In monumental words of Christ we feel love pouring into the hearts of human beings:

> Where two or three are gathered together
> in my name, there am I in the midst of them.

In like manner the ancient Rosicrucian saying resounds into the love that is wedded with wisdom: *In Christo Morimur,* In Christ we die.

Through Jehovah, human beings were predestined for a group-soul existence; love was to penetrate into them gradually through blood-relationship. It is through Lucifer that the human being lives as a personality. Originally, therefore, human beings were in a state of union, then of separateness as a consequence of the luciferic principle that promotes selfishness, independence. Together with selfishness, evil came into the world. It had to be so, because without the evil, human beings could not lay hold of the good. When human beings gain victory over themselves, the unfolding of love is possible. Christ brought the impulse for this victory to humans in the clutches of increasing egoism, and thereby the power to conquer evil. The acts of Christ bring together again the human beings who were separated through egoism and selfishness. The words of Christ concerning acts of love are true in the very deepest sense:

> *Inasmuch as you have done it to one of the least of these my brethren, you have done it to me.*

The divine act of love flowed back upon the Earth; as time goes on, in spite of the forces of physical decay and death, the evolution of humankind will be permeated and imbued with new spiritual life through this act—a deed performed not out of egoism, but solely out of the spirit of love. *Per Spiritum Sanctum Reviviscimus,* Through the Holy Spirit we live again.

Yet the future of humanity will consist of something besides love. Spiritual perfecting will be for earthly human beings the most worthy goal to aspire to (this is described at the beginning of my second Mystery drama, *The Soul's Probation*), but none who understand what acts of love truly are will say that their own striving for perfection is selfless. Striving for perfection imparts strength to our being and to our personality.

But our value for the world must be seen to lie wholly in acts of love, not in what is done for the sake of self-perfecting. Let us be under no illusion about this. When a person is endeavoring to follow Christ through love of wisdom and dedicates that wisdom to the service of the world, it only takes real effect to the extent it is filled with love.

Wisdom steeped in love, which at once furthers the world and leads the world to Christ—this love of wisdom also excludes the lie. For the lie is the direct opposite of the actual facts, and those who yield themselves lovingly to the facts are incapable of lying. The lie has its roots in egoism—always and without exception. When, through love, we have found the path to wisdom, we reach wisdom through the increasing power of self-conquest, through selfless love. In this way the human being becomes a free individuality. The evil was the subsoil into which the light of love was able to shine; but it is love that enables us to grasp the meaning and place of evil in the world. The darkness has enabled the light to come into our ken. Only a person who is free in the real sense can become a true Christian.

EPILOGUE

I-Feeling, the Soul's Capacity to Love, and Their Relationship to the Elemental World

from *The Threshold of the Spiritual World*

WHEN the human soul consciously enters the elemental world, it finds itself compelled to change many of the ideas it gained in the sense-perceptible world. If you have strengthened the soul's powers appropriately, you will be able to make such changes. Indeed, you *must* attain that strength of soul and not shy away from doing so. Otherwise, when you enter the elemental world, you will be overwhelmed by the feeling that you are losing the solid ground needed to build up your inner life will. The ideas you gained in the physical world will not impede your entry into the elemental world unless you hold onto them as tightly as you did when you gained them in the sense-perceptible world.

You cling to these ideas only because your soul is *habituated* to doing so. For a consciousness that initially experienced only the sense world it is completely natural that it should become accustomed to taking the form of ideas that it developed there as the only one possible. In fact, it is more than natural; it is *necessary.* The life of the soul would never achieve the inner unity and the stability it needed, if it did not develop its consciousness in a sense-perceptible world ruled by fixed and necessary ideas. Everything given to the soul through living with the sense-perceptible world enables it to enter the elemental world without losing its independent, self-contained, and stable nature.

Thus, we must strengthen and empower our soul life. Then, when the soul enters the elemental world, its independence is not just present unconsciously; rather, it is there as something that is held clearly and consciously. If the soul is too weak to experience the elemental world consciously, then, when it enters that world, its independence disappears, just as a thought disappears when impressed so feebly upon the soul that it does not live on in the memory. A soul of this kind cannot enter the supersensible world consciously. Each time it tries to enter, the being in the soul (whom we call the "Guardian of the Threshold") throws it back into the sense-perceptible world. And if, in the attempt, the soul gets a taste of the supersensible world and, after sinking back into the sense-perceptible world, still retains some recollection of the supersensible world, then this prize from another realm can confuse our thinking. It is, however, quite impossible to fall into such confusion if we cultivate the kind of healthy power of judgment that we can acquire in the sense-perceptible world.

By strengthening our powers of judgment, we develop the proper relationship of the soul to the processes and beings of the supersensible worlds. To live in those worlds consciously, your soul must possess a natural tendency that it cannot develop as fully in the sense world as it can in the supersensible worlds: namely, the tendency of *devotion to what one experiences.* You must dive down into experience; you must be able to *unite* with it. You must be able to do that to such a degree that you see yourself outside your own nature and feel yourself within another.

Your own being must *transform* into the one you are experiencing. Without this capacity for transformation, you cannot experience anything genuine in the supersensible worlds. For the basis of all experience in the supersensible world is the conscious knowledge: "Now I have transformed myself in a particular way. I am united vitally with another being whose nature has thus transformed me."

To transform oneself in this way—to feel oneself into another being—is to live in the supersensible worlds. Thereby, you come to know the beings and processes of those worlds. You notice how you relate to one being in this way or that, and differently to another whose nature is further from your own. Distinct shades of experiences arise—especially in the elemental world—that you could characterize as sympathy and antipathy. For instance, when meeting an elemental being or process, you may feel an experience arising in your soul that you can characterize as sympathetic. Through this experience of sympathy, you come to understand the nature of that elemental being or process.

Do not imagine, however, that these experiences of sympathy or antipathy occur only in varying strengths or degrees of intensity. True, in the physical world, in a certain sense one speaks of experiences of sympathy and antipathy *only* as being stronger or weaker. But in the elemental world, you can differentiate sympathies and antipathies not only by their strength, but also by their color, just as we can distinguish colors from one another in the sense world. We experience the sense world as many-colored. Likewise, we can experience the elemental world as manifoldly sympathetic or antipathetic. Here, we must remember, too, that in the realm of elemental beings "antipathetic" does *not* connote that we inwardly turn away from something. "Antipathetic" simply refers to a characteristic of an elemental being or process that relates to a sympathetic characteristic of another process or being, as the color blue relates to red in the sense-perceptible world.

We can speak of a "sense" that people can awaken in their etheric bodies for seeing the elemental world. That sense can perceive sympathies and antipathies in the elemental world, just as the eye perceives colors or the ear tones in the sense world. Just as in the sense-perceptible world one object is red and another blue, to spiritual sight, some beings of the elemental world radiate a kind of sympathy and others a kind of antipathy.

This experience of the elemental world through sympathy and antipathy, again, does not occur only to the supersensibly awakened soul. It is *always* present in every human soul; indeed, it belongs to the being of the human soul. In ordinary soul life, however, knowledge of this part of human nature is not developed. People have within them an etheric body, and this connects them in hundreds of ways with the beings and processes of the elemental world. At one moment we are interwoven with certain sympathies and antipathies in the elemental world and at another moment, with others.

Now, the soul cannot live constantly as an etheric being so that the sympathies and antipathies are always active there in a clearly articulated way. In sense-perceptible existence, the states of waking and sleeping must alternate; likewise, in the elemental world, the soul's experience of sympathies and antipathies must have an opposite state. The soul can withdraw from all sympathies and antipathies and inwardly experience only itself, that is, consider and feel only its own being. That feeling can become so intense that we can speak of "willing" our own being.

Here, it is a question of a state of the soul's life not easily described, because in its pure, original nature this state is such that there is nothing like it in the sense-perceptible world other than the soul's strong, pure sense of "self" or I-feeling. We can describe that state in the elemental world by saying that, as far as the necessary devotion to experiences of sympathy and antipathy is concerned, the soul feels the urge to say to itself "*I will be wholly for me; only in me.*"

Only by a kind of *unfolding of the will* can the soul wrench itself from its state of devotion to the experiences of sympathy and antipathy in the elemental world. In the elemental world, this living-in-oneself is like the state of sleep, whereas devotion to processes and beings corresponds to the waking state.

If the soul is awake in the elemental world and develops the will to experience itself— that is, feels a need for "elemental sleep"—it can achieve that by returning to the waking state of sense life with a fully developed feeling of self. For the experience of the sense world, when saturated by the feeling of self, is precisely elemental sleep. It is the freeing of the soul from elemental experiences. It is literally true that, for supersensible consciousness, the life of the soul in the sense-perceptible world is spiritual sleep.

A person who has developed spiritual vision in the right way, and awakens in the supersensible world, retains the memory of soul experiences in the sense world. If you did not retain that memory, other beings and processes would be present in your clairvoyant consciousness, but not your own being. You would then have no knowledge of your self. You yourself would not live spiritually, but other beings and processes would live in your soul. Thinking this through, you will understand why a properly developed clairvoyant must place significant value upon developing a strong "I-feeling."

The I-feeling developed in connection with clairvoyance definitely does not arise initially in the soul through clairvoyance. Clairvoyance simply helps us learn to recognize what was always present in the depths of our soul, but remained unconscious for ordinary, sensory life.

This strong "I-feeling" does not come about through the etheric body as such, but through the soul's experience of the physical-sensory body. If the soul does not bring this I-feeling—developed through its experiences in the sense-perceptible world—into the clairvoyant state, it will soon become evident that the soul is not adequately prepared for the experience of the elemental world.

Yet, human consciousness in the sense world requires that the soul's self-feeling (its I-experience), although present, be muted. This gives the soul the opportunity in the sense world to experience the training for the noblest moral force, *empathy or compassion.* If a strong sense of self were to dominate the soul's conscious experiences in the sense-perceptible world, then moral instincts and ideas could not properly develop. They could not bring forth the fruit of *love.*

Devotion (the natural impulse in the elemental world) is not the same as what we call *love* in normal human experience. Elemental devotion is based upon an experience of oneself in another being or process; love is an experience of the other in one's own soul. To experience love, however, a sort of veil must be drawn in the soul over the self-feeling (I-experience) present in its depths. Then, because its own powers are muted, the joys and sorrows of the other arise in the soul. And so, love, which is the source of the most genuine moral impulse in human life, germinates.

Love is for us the most important fruit of human experience in the sense-perceptible world. If you penetrate the nature of love, or compassion, you will discover how the spiritual expresses itself in its truth in the sense-perceptible world. I have already said that it is part of supersensible nature to transform itself into something else. If the spiritual in physical human life transforms itself in such a way that the sense of self is muted, and rises as love, then the spiritual remains true to its own elemental laws. We can say that, with supersensible consciousness, the human soul awakens in the spiritual world. But, we must also say that, *through love, the spirit awakens in the sense-perceptible world.* Wherever love and compassion are active in life, we can perceive the magic breath of the spirit blowing through the sense world.

Therefore, when properly developed, clairvoyance never blunts love or compassion. The more the soul becomes accustomed in the right way to the spiritual worlds, the more it will feel lovelessness and the lack of empathy and compassion as *a denial of the spirit itself.*

Consciousness experiences that lead to clairvoyance demonstrate quite particular characteristics. The I-feeling required for experience in the supersensible worlds is easily muted. Often, it is like a weak, glimmering memory. But at the same time, as soon as one enters the supersensible world, feelings of hate or lovelessness and immoral impulses become strong soul experiences. They present themselves to the soul as accusations that have come alive; they become horribly real pictures. In order not to be tortured by those pictures, supersensible consciousness often searches for spiritual forces that can weaken their impressions. But these powers then permeate the soul with forces that can spoil the clairvoyance one has gained. The forces drive clairvoyance away from the good realms of the spiritual world and direct it toward the bad.

On the other hand, genuine love and true soul kindness are experiences that strengthen consciousness, giving it the forces needed to enter into clairvoyance. I said that we must prepare the soul before it can have supersensible experiences. It must be added that a genuine capacity for love and a desire for true human kindness, compassion, and empathy are among the many means of such preparation.

An overdeveloped I-feeling in the physical world works against morality. A too weakly developed I-feeling lacks inner certainty and stability. It surrounds the soul with storms of elemental sympathies and antipathies. Inner certainty and stability can be there only when a sufficiently strong I-feeling works from experiences in the physical sensory world into the etheric body (although this remains unknown to us in normal life). To develop a genuinely moral attitude in our souls, we must mute our I-feeling with tendencies toward compassion and love.

* * *

The Boundary between the Sense-Perceptible and the Supersensible Worlds

Observing the cosmos, spiritual science sees in *egotism* the origin of "evil" in human activity. You would misunderstand "cosmic order" if you were to believe that this order could exist without the forces that form the source of evil. If these powers were not present, the etheric human being could not develop in the elemental world. Indeed, so long as they operate *only* in the elemental world, such forces are thoroughly good. They become the cause of *evil* when they do not remain in the depths of the soul, where they can regulate the relationship of the human being to the elemental world, but enter the soul's experiences in the sense world, transforming themselves into egotistic impulses. They then act against the capacity to love, and become the origin of immoral activity.

* * *

On the Nature of the Spiritual Worlds

...Luciferic beings act in a *liberating* way upon the human soul. They raise the soul above simply being interwoven with the sense-perceptible world. But if we allow into the *physical world* the soul life that should unfold only in the *elemental world*—if we allow our physical feelings to be influenced by antipathies and sympathies that should prevail only in the etheric body—then, by means of this misplaced soul life, luciferic beings gain an influence contrary to universal cosmic order. Such luciferic influence is especially present wherever the sympathies and antipathies of the sense-perceptible world contain something other than love based upon compassion for the life of another sense-perceptible being. If you can love a person because he or she meets you with some characteristic or another, then no luciferic element can mix into that love. Love that is founded upon qualities occurring in sense existence keeps its distance from the luciferic element. Love that is *not* grounded in the beloved in this way, but grounded instead in the person loving, tends toward a luciferic influence. If you love someone because he or she has qualities toward which your nature, as the one who loves, tends, you love that person with that part of the soul that luciferic elements can approach.

Consequently, we should never say that luciferic elements are always evil, because the human soul must love the processes and beings of the supersensible worlds *luciferically*. A contradiction to cosmic order occurs only when we direct toward the sense-perceptible world the kind of love with which we should instead feel ourselves drawn toward the supersensible world. A love for the supersensible rightly evokes a heightened sense of self in the loving being. But love sought in the sense-perceptible world for the sake of such an increased sense of self corresponds to a luciferic temptation. When sought for the sake of self, love of the spiritual acts to *free*. But, love of the sense-perceptible, when sought for one's own sake, does not act to free. Rather, it confines the self through the gratification it obtains.

Ahrimanic beings become apparent in the thinking soul in much the same way that luciferic beings appear in the feeling soul. They confine thinking to the sense-perceptible world. They divert it from the fact that thoughts have meaning only when they appear as part of the great order of cosmic thought, which cannot be found in sense-perceptible existence.

The ahrimanic element must exist in the world, into which human soul life is woven, as a necessary counterweight to the luciferic. Without the luciferic element, the soul would dream away its life, observing sense-perceptible existence. It would find no reason to rise above it. Without the counteraction of the ahrimanic element, the soul would fall prey to the luciferic. It would give very little significance to the sense-perceptible world, despite the fact that some of the conditions necessary for its existence are in that world. It would have no desire to learn about the sense-perceptible world. The ahrimanic element acquires its proper meaning in the human soul when it leads to a life in the world that is appropriate to it, when we accept it for what it is and forgo everything in it that is of a transitory nature. It is quite impossible to say that to avoid falling victim to the luciferic and ahrimanic elements, one should eradicate them in oneself.

***

Three Prayers for the Dead

from *Unsere Toten*

1.

May my heart's love become soul love,
may my love's warmth stream to spirit
light—
thus I would draw near to you:
thinking spirit thoughts with you
feeling world love in you
willing in spirit through you,
weaving being united in experience.

(for Rudolf Hahn, following the death of his wife)

2.

May my love be woven
as offering
into the sheaths now surrounding
you—
may my love
cool your heat
warm your cold—
may you live
carried by love
showered by light
upward.

3.

My soul's love
my love's
meaning
strive toward you—
they wish to bear you
they wish to hold you
in the heights of hope
in the spheres of love.

Further Reading

Works by Rudolf Steiner

Anthroposophical Leading Thoughts. London: Rudolf Steiner Press, 1998.

Anthroposophy (A Fragment): A New Foundation for the Study of Human Nature. Hudson, NY: Anthroposophic Press, 1996.

Anthroposophy and the Inner Life. Bristol, UK: Rudolf Steiner Press, 1994.

At the Gates of Spiritual Science. London: Rudolf Steiner Press, 1986.

Christianity as Mystical Fact. Hudson, NY: Anthroposophic Press, 1997.

The Christian Mystery. Hudson, NY: Anthroposophic Press, 1998.

The Christmas Conference for the Foundation of the General Anthroposophical Society 1923–1924. Hudson, NY: Anthroposophic Press, 1990.

Cosmic Memory. Blauvelt, NY: Garber Communications, 1990.

The Effects of Esoteric Development. Hudson, NY: Anthroposophic Press, 1997.

The Evolution of Consciousness as Revealed through Initiation-Knowledge. Sussex, UK: Rudolf Steiner Press, 1991.

The Fall of the Spirits of Darkness. London: Rudolf Steiner Press, 1995.

The Foundations of Human Experience. Hudson, NY: Anthroposophic Press, 1996 (previous translation titled *Study of Man*).

The Foundation Stone & The Life, Nature and Cultivation of Anthroposophy. London: Rudolf Steiner Press, 1996.

The Four Mystery Plays. London: Rudolf Steiner Press, 1983.

Goethe's World View. Spring Valley, NY: Mercury Press, 1985.

The Gospel of St. John. Hudson, NY: Anthroposophic Press, 1988.

Guidance in Esoteric Training: From the Esoteric School. London: Rudolf Steiner Press, 1998.

How to Know Higher Worlds. Hudson, NY: Anthroposophic Press, 1994.

Human and Cosmic Thought. London: Rudolf Steiner Press, 1991.

Individualism in Philosophy. Spring Valley, NY: Mercury Press, 1989.

Mysticism at the Dawn of the Modern Age. Blauvelt, NY: Rudolf Steiner Publications, 1960.

Polarities in the Evolution of Mankind. London: Rudolf Steiner Press, 1987.

A Way of Self-Knowledge. Hudson, NY: Anthroposophic Press, 1998.

Rudolf Steiner, An Autobiography. Blauvelt, NY: Garber Communications, 1977.

Spiritual Beings in the Heavenly Bodies and in the Kingdoms of Nature. Hudson, NY: Anthroposophic Press, 1992.

The Spiritual Guidance of the Individual and Humanity. Hudson, NY: Anthroposophic Press, 1992.

The Spiritual Hierarchies and the Physical World: Reality and Illusion. Hudson, NY: Anthroposophic Press, 1996.

The Temple Legend: Freemasonry and Related Occult Movements. London: Rudolf Steiner Press, 1997.

Theosophy. Hudson, NY: Anthroposophic Press, 1994.

Truth and Knowledge. Blauvelt, NY: Rudolf Steiner Publications, 1981. Also *Truth and Science.* Spring Valley, NY: Mercury Press, 1993.

Works by Other Authors

Barnes, Henry. *A Life for the Spirit: Rudolf Steiner in the Crosscurrents of Our Time.* Hudson, NY: Anthroposophic Press, 1997.

Burkhard, Gudrun. *Taking Charge: Your Life Patterns and Their Meaning.* Edinburgh: Floris Books, 1992.

Easton, Stewart. *New Vistas in Psychology: An Anthroposophical Contribution.* London: Rudolf Steiner Press, 1984.

Gädeke, Wolfgang. *Sexuality, Partnership and Marriage: From a Spiritual Perspective.* London: Temple Lodge, 1998.

Kühlewind, Georg. *From Normal to Healthy: Paths to the Liberation of Consciousness.* Hudson, NY: Lindisfarne Books, 1988.

Lowndes, Florin. *Enlivening the Chakra of the Heart: The Fundamental Spiritual Exercises of Rudolf Steiner.* London: Sophia Books, 1993.

Maclean, Dorothy. *Choices of Love.* Hudson, NY: Lindisfarne Books, 1998.

McDermott, Robert (ed.). *The Essential Steiner.* San Francisco: HarperSanFrancisco, 1984.

Nesfield-Cookson, Bernard. *Michael and the Two-Horned Beast: The Challenge of Evil Today in the Light of Rudolf Steiner's Science of the Spirit.* London: Temple Lodge, 1998.

——— *Rudolf Steiner's Vision of Love: Spiritual Science and the Logic of the Heart.* London: Rudolf Steiner Press, 1994.

Prokofieff, Sergei. *The Occult Significance of Forgiveness.* London: Temple Lodge Publishing, 1995.

Querido, René (ed). *A Western Approach to Reincarnation and Karma: Selected Lectures and Writings by Rudolf Steiner.* Hudson, NY: Anthroposophic Press, 1996.

Richards, M.C. *Opening Our Moral Eye: Essays, Talks, and Poems Embracing Creativity and Community.* Hudson, NY: Lindisfarne Books, 1996.

Sardello, Robert. *Facing the World with Soul: The Reimagination of Modern Life.* Hudson, NY: Lindisfarne Books, 1992.

Seddon, Richard. *Mani, His Life and Work: Transforming Evil.* London: Temple Lodge, 1998.

Sleigh, Julian. *Friends and Lovers: Working through Relationships.* Edinburgh: Floris Books, 1998.

Smit, Jörgen. *How to Transform Thinking, Feeling, and Willing: Practical exercises for the training of thinking, feeling, willing, imagination, composure, intuition, positivity, and wonder.* Stroud, UK: Hawthorn Press, 1988.

Solovyov, Vladimir. *Lectures on Divine Humanity.* Hudson, NY: Lindisfarne Books, 1995.

——— *The Meaning of Love*. Hudson, NY: Lindisfarne Books, 1985.

Staley, Betty. *Tapestries: Weaving Life's Journey*. Stroud, UK: Hawthorn Press, 1997.

Sussman, Linda. *Speech of the Grail: A Journey toward Speaking that Heals and Transforms*. Hudson, NY: Lindisfarne Books, 1995.

Wachsmuth, Guenther. *The Life and Work of Rudolf Steiner*. Blauvelt, NY: Garber Communications, 1989.

During the last two decades of the nineteenth century Austrian-born Rudolf Steiner (1861–1925) became a respected and well-published scientific, literary, and philosophical scholar, particularly known for his work on Goethe's scientific writings. After the turn of the century he began to develop his earlier philosophical principles into an approach to methodical research of psychological and spiritual phenomena.

His multifaceted genius has led to innovative and holistic approaches in medicine, science, education (Waldorf schools), special education, philosophy, religion, economics, agriculture (Biodynamic method), architecture, drama, the new arts of eurythmy and speech, and other fields. In 1924 he founded the General Anthroposophical Society, which today has branches throughout the world.

. . . .

For an informative catalog of the work of Rudolf Steiner and other anthroposophical authors please contact